D1559352

MARTHA, MARY, AND JESUS

WEAVING ACTION AND CONTEMPLATION IN DAILY LIFE

Nancy Corson Carter

A Liturgical Press Book

THE LITURGICAL PRESS
Collegeville, Minnesota

Cover design by Ann Blattner

Cover illustration: ''Jesus at the house of Martha and Mary'' by Gustave Doré

1   2   3   4   5   6   7   8   9

Library of Congress Cataloging-in-Publication Data

Carter, Nancy Corson, 1943–
    Martha, Mary, and Jesus : weaving action and contemplation in daily life   /
    Nancy Corson Carter.
        p.   cm.
    Includes bibliographical references.
    ISBN 0-8146-2119-8
    1. Christian life—1960- 2. Carter, Nancy Corson, 1943- —Religion.
    3. Martha, Saint. 4. Mary, of Bethany, Saint. 5. Contemplation.
    6. Intention—Religious aspects—Christianity.
    I. Title.
    BV4501.2.C3354   1992
    248.4—dc20   92-23586
                                                                          CIP

Contents

Acknowledgments

As I begin to think of those to whom I am indebted in this work, I am both delighted and chagrined to realize just how deeply we are, each one of us, dependent upon a vast web of intricately interconnected collaborators. I give thanks to them all and name a few specially shining strands.

Without the extraordinary opportunity afforded me by the Coolidge Colloquium in Boston, June 1985, this study would not exist. I have deep gratitude for its patron, Mr. William Appleton Coolidge, for its sponsor, the Association for Religion and Intellectual Life, and for all my inspiring and supportive colleagues there. I owe special thanks to Tony Stoneburner, Elena Malits, Carol Ochs, and Dana Greene.

My thanks for the sustaining friendships of the Rev. Lacy R. Harwell, Elaine Prevallet, S.L., the Very Rev. LeRoy D. Lawson, the Rev. Ann Graham, and Nancy Appunn. My thanks to Dr. John Draeger for his Greek New Testament classes and to Jean Lersch for her guidance in journaling with Scripture. My abiding thanks to the congregation of Maximo Presbyterian Church, St. Petersburg, Florida. The loving encouragement of the women's retreat group at Maximo has been a great boon to me.

Thanks to the Rev. Janet Williams Banker and the Rev. Karen Johnson for sharing their sermons about Martha and Mary. I celebrate the Rev. Barbara A. B. Patterson for being a special friend to me and the Martha-Mary work during a sabbatical at Emory University.

I am grateful to Eckerd College for support through Faculty Development Grants and through the typing assistance of Letters Office work scholars and secretary Shirley Davis. My thanks to Marti Patchell for her assistance while I worked at Georgetown University. Helen Coleman's excellent editing gave the manuscript new life when it most needed it.

And last, but never least, my loving gratitude to my parents, Dorothy and Harvey F. Corson, for life-long encouragement, to my mother-in-law, Marjorie Carter, for her unfailing enthusiasm, to my daughter Rebecca, for her spirited support, and to my husband Howard, for unstinting hours of editing, listening, and faithful companioning.

Introduction

Without deluding ourselves about achieving immortality, we need to act freely and sometimes boldly to express ourselves in ways that offer our gifts to others (Parker Palmer, *The Active Life,* 20).

I offer this book in the spirit of "the gift must move." Though I do not claim to be an Everywoman/Everyman, I have received a gift in the writing of this book that seems not just mine. The stories, the guiding metaphors of weaving and household, the process of trying to allow one's life to become more and more open to the sacred through learning how to best combine prayer and contemplation with right action, all these seem *ours.*

The New Testament stories of Martha, Mary, and Jesus have helped me to understand that I am *both* Martha and Mary and that with Jesus' help I can be complete in this *in my everyday life.* I began the study because I had difficulty even imagining that I could reconcile the Martha and Mary within me—they had been in conflict for so long. Quite simplistically at first, Martha represented dutiful action and Mary represented quiet contemplation. Owing to my upbringing in the 1940s as a dutiful oldest daughter/child, I internalized a set of stereotypical rules for women (which had their analogues for men as well): if I wanted to be Mary, I had best enter a convent (for men, a monastery or the ministry); if I wanted to get married, have a family, possibly even work outside the home (a requirement for men), then Martha was the model I had to follow.

But I was a troublesomely "mixed" person, and I was left feeling divided and frustrated because of this. Years later, when I had already entered deeply into the very Martha-like American world of work and family, in my early 40s, I felt an urge to give Mary her due. So what follows is an account of the issues I met as I resolved to use the Martha, Mary, and Jesus stories as guides toward reconciling insights. In this work I chronicle my way toward understanding that Martha and Mary are *sisters*, forever related in one family household. This is a way that is especially sensitive to these issues as women meet them, but I intend it, as I have indicated, also as a companioning way for men. In *The Active Life*, a study by Parker Palmer that deals insightfully with these same issues, I find affirmation for the central idea of this project: "Rather than speak of contemplation and action, we might speak of contemplation-and-action, letting the hyphens suggest what our language obscures: that the one cannot exist without the other" (15). You will find in this book that I believe this is true within the lives of individuals and also within the lives of human communities.

Reading Palmer's book has been helpful in focusing my own ideas about contemplation and action. Whereas he writes from the viewpoint of one who has discovered, at last, that he is primarily an active person and "not a monk," I write more from the viewpoint of one who has lately discovered 1) that I am primarily a contemplative (Mary) person despite my emphasis in recent years on the active (Martha) life and 2) that I had a lot of work to do in clarifying who Martha was before I could rightly claim Mary. That recognition led me further into studying just how interdependent Mary and Martha are in human nature, starting from my own perspective, and how important it was that I follow them through into a broader, more mature contexting of faith and life.

Of all the scholars and writers I cite to emphasize the interdependency of Martha and Mary in the final chapter, "Prayer as Context," perhaps it is Gerald G. May who most succinctly states the case for our developing *both*: "To pray as if all depends on divine action is to support passivity and self-suppression. To labor as if all depended on our own effort is to court willfulness in a dangerous way . . . it is *both* that are demanded if one's spiritual journey is to be meaningfully reflected in life" (208–09).

There is a question that hides behind the epigraph I have chosen for this chapter: Is it the human condition to be burdened with a curious mixture of humility and arrogance? If, as I believe, it *is*, then I admit my humanness at the very beginning: at once I feel humbled to write so much in first person, and at the same time I am bold enough to believe that I have learned lessons and gathered materials here that are to be shared. I think of one of my literary heroes, Henry David Thoreau, who had utmost faith that his "I" was connected with the universal. As he wrote in the second paragraph of *Walden*, "We commonly do not remember that it is, after all, always the first person that is speaking. I should not talk so much about myself if there were anybody else whom I knew as well. . . . I, on my side, require of every writer, first or last, a simple and sincere account of his [or her!] own life, and not merely what he had heard of other men's lives . . ." (3).

Though he felt that perhaps "poor students" were his most particular audience for that work, still he felt as I do in my weaving/writing: "I trust that none will stretch the seams in putting on the coat, for it may do good service to him [her] whom it fits" (4).

When I began this writing, I was in search of a guiding story. Furthermore, I dimly understood that I was seeking transformation; I was somehow to take the tangled threads of my personal life and weave a web that held meaning for a life opening out into the communal/universal. My quest was to embrace a rebirth from the ego-centered first half of my life into the transpersonally oriented second half of my life. I first heard this transition articulated by the psychologist C. G. Jung; he had written wisely of our need at mid-life to turn from life's necessary concentration upon perpetuation of the physical life

to an equally necessary concentration upon the symbolic birthing of our psychic/spiritual life, in order to become fully developed selves (17ff.).

In other words, I am talking about coming to that time in
life when our children, literal or figurative, are independent
enough not to need much of our young-child-parenting ener-
gies. We have energy to spare and experience to share. What
needs to be birthed/mended/healed in our own and contingent
worlds?

In the way of all grace-filled synchronicity, the stories of
Jesus, Martha, and Mary in the New Testament Gospels of
Luke and John appealed to me with a seductive luminosity (I
might even have used the word "erotic" instead of "seductive," meaning that I sought knowledge alive with human connections, not simply elegant abstractions). These stories, and
especially the one in Luke which contrasts Martha's anxious
activity with Mary's quiet listening at Jesus' feet, spoke directly
to me.

Though my own motivation to explore these stories was
many-faceted, I believe it was the Christian/feminist/ecologist
part of me that most directly responded. I felt myself and
others, the Earth as well, abused by false hierarchies, by mis-
leading values of progress, productivity, and power. In terms
of the Martha-Mary dichotomy I felt in myself, I saw Western, American culture as overemphasizing a male Martha-ness.
The culture-shaping "male Marthas" exhibited qualities of
decisive, action-oriented, quick-acting, and aggressive control
over and against "wimpy Marys," that is, the ones who dared
to be vulnerable to multiple points of view (even those of non-
humans and the Earth itself) and to endure periods of patient
waiting for clarity, who could go slowly when this was needed
(even though it looked like weakness), who could imagine not
being right just because they had technological, economic, and
political/military power. (Reading Riane Eisler's *The Chalice and
the Blade*, I find that her contrast of a "domination model,"
which she suggests we need to jettison, with a "partnership
model," which she urges us to embrace [xvii] is allied to my

own feelings about the shift we Earthlings must make if we are to survive.)

I felt a pressing need to *do something* to contribute to a change in these values, but I knew that this doing had to be based in a far greater love and wisdom than I alone possessed. I knew my rising indignation could lead to angry acts and words, ones that would not bring the kind of change I wanted. So I was looking for a lifeline. When I encountered the Martha, Mary, and Jesus stories, they seemed like an Ariadne cord leading out of the dark and monster-controlled labyrinth. Between Martha's action and Mary's contemplation I intuited a way that might open outward to Light; somehow I *knew* that the Holy Spirit would guide me if I persevered in pondering their stories.

I note that throughout the weaving/writing I often address issues involved with spirituality and feminism, but the theme of ecology implicitly undergirds it all: How may we best serve as keepers and healers of God's magnificent Creation, acting in our "local household" with the "global household" in mind? How may we engage in a patient process akin to weaving that daily increases human-Creation harmony? Since we have recently been a nation at war, I have an even greater sense of urgency about finding non-violent ways for humans to live on the Earth. Surely we all, as seekers, feel poignantly called to effectively combine prayer/contemplation and right action in these troubling times.

I had the unusual good fortune to first weave this Mary-Martha material as a member of the Coolidge Colloquium, a program of Associates for Religion and Intellectual Life. We were twenty-five Jewish and Christian participants invited "to work on an individual project at the intersection of intellectual and religious concerns (grounded in a religious tradition) and to share in dialogue and worship together." For the month of June 1985 at Andover Newton Theological School in Boston we had an invigorating opportunity to pursue our solitary work within the context of a community sharing meals, worship, and continuing conversation. During that time I struggled to understand the Mary and Martha stories in my own and others' lives;

it was a struggle to understand my own creative process as well, especially as it became more consciously linked with my spiritual journey. I have an abiding gratitude for this time of "dressing the loom," for the enlivening support of all my scholar-weaver-friends there.

I am grateful not only for the Colloquium experience, but also for other experiences in my life that have trained me to consider crucial issues within the context of a faith tradition. My first understanding of the power of connecting faith and intellect came to me as a confirmand under the tutelage of my pastor at St. Andrew's Lutheran Church in Muncy, Pennsylvania, the Rev. Louis K. Helldorfer. I earned my B.A. at a Lutheran liberal arts college, Susquehanna University, which then had required faith and ethics courses, as well as daily chapel; after graduation I spent half a summer in Europe studying art, theology, and philosophy on a tour with an S.U. Professor of Religion, Otto Reimherr. When I went off to graduate school, my mother found a wonderful place for me to stay: the Lutheran student center, Christus House, in Iowa City; I met my husband-to-be singing in Daniel Moe's choir at Gloria Dei Lutheran Church, Iowa City. One of my most inspiring teachers at the University of Iowa was Sidney E. Mead, Professor of American Church History. I have been teaching since 1972 at Eckerd College, formerly Florida Presbyterian College; there I've been involved in such faith-tradition-evaluating courses as "Search for Spirit" and "Judaeo-Christian Perspectives on Contemporary Issues." I have become an elder in nearby Maximo Presbyterian Church.

My work at the Colloquium grew out of this rich background. As the initial setting for this study, it demanded that I consider the solitary weaving in connection with community. Naturally, then, I came to link the metaphor of weaving with one of household; what was appearing in the work was the clear message that the weaving represented for me a rededication of life and work within community. My growing understanding, woven of a matrix that combined the solitary and the communal, was to be expressed as an account of a process of attending to a sacred story which invites and allows transformation.

In using the two companion metaphors of weaving and household, I wish to suggest a process which enables us increasingly to practice the presence of God where we live here and now, in every moment—with the fullness of our combined active and contemplative selves—and to enter, as I believe Martha and Mary did with Jesus, into communal co-creation with the Spirit. In choosing the metaphor of household, I declare my belief that this work is "homely," it is the stuff of humble persons in the mundane activities of daily life, and not only of priests and priestesses before incense-fogged high altars.

Throughout the book I weave back and forth between what is personal and what is communal. I use journal entries and dialogues to indicate how this work begins on an intimate, individual level; and then, using the metaphor of household, I indicate how this personal insight, gained through working with one's own inner material, may lead outward toward fuller, deeper service with others. The dialogue form serves me well as I seek to understand how the Martha and Mary parts of me and the Martha and Mary parts of communities function: what are their bases for conflict and what are their bases for working together? Basically, it means to me as teacher and as person that I have found a way to settle some issues that kept me ego-occupied, unable to attend to others' needs; and I have found some ways to help others make this same transition from self-occupation toward more openness to others, having at once more patience and more compassion about the difficulty of this work. I feel that I have found ways for the Martha and Mary within me to end their conflict and to find a dynamic harmony; this has led to a re-visioning of how the Martha and Mary elements of community may likewise rejoice in their complementarity. Throughout this work I have felt deep gratitude toward those who companion and support me as the "cloud of believers," the "beloved community," the "body of Christ."

At first I resisted the very personal first part of this process;

it seemed, in fact, too "feminine"—an overworking of the feminist motto of "the personal is the political" into the spiritual/theological realm. However, over time, I learned that this stage of the process was as necessary as crawling before walking is to a baby. As I have said, Thoreau is one of my exemplars; he and the other American transcendentalists have given me an understanding that is basic to this work: when we are most honestly, most deeply personal, we reach into the realm of the universal/transcendent. I re-learn the truth of this each time I teach my Writing Workshop course called "Journals, Diaries, and Letters: the Intimate Connection" (a course inspired in part by our use of journals in a team-taught course once in Eckerd College's curriculum called "Search for Spirit"). As my students and I share our writings and as we read already published journals by famous and not-famous persons, we often find our own experiences validated. We see that we are not alone in some of our most troubling experiences; others have gone before and have found ways to survive and sometimes even be ennobled by them. Nor are we alone in our most joyous moments; in them we join a great circle of celebration. So my "I" is an invitation to your "I"; consider us shuttling our threads through one enormous tapestry that requires all of us to weave as well as we are able if the design is to be complete.

As I combed the yarn of my own childhood in rural Pennsylvania and of my own educational/spiritual path, I found important clues to the shape this weaving had already been taking. Like the *prima materia* of the medieval alchemists, I found that this matter of our lives is what we each have to work with; no matter how base our own little pile of thread at first appears to us, it is *basic*, and through the guiding hand of the Holy Spirit, the Holy Spinster of this work, it may become part of a great communal web or network.

I also rejoice in the discovery that through this process *each* of us is invited to fully use her/his unique ways of expression. My pattern of perception and expression often follows a model that is more webbed or spiralled than conventional linear ones; I recently was heartened to read Leslie Marmon Silko, a Native

American writer, telling of the Pueblo way of communicating: "[T]he structure of Pueblo expression resembles something like a spider's web—with many little threads radiating from a center, criss-crossing each other. As with the web, the structure will emerge as it is made and you must simply listen and trust, as the Pueblo people do, that meaning will be made" (54).

I am by nature a kindred spinner; using the metaphor of weaving gives me new ways to manifest this nature. I know that this is not haphazard work, but a weaving constructed according to an organic pattern based on a definite center (a pattern not easily visible to ones unaccustomed to such weaving, but a *teachable/learnable* pattern nevertheless, an assumption of this study). My Ph.D. in American Civilization is an interdisciplinary degree, and much of my teaching crosses standard disciplinary lines. As an environmentalist I realize that there is no natural division between what we call "economics," "agronomy," "biology," "marine science," "ecology," or any other field that guides the human-nature relationship. (What field, in fact, can be exempt when the real "field" is the entire planet?) Naturally then, this study is interdisciplinary in both content and form. Theology, art, myth, and literature are among the "fields" interwoven here. This content is interwoven with similar varied forms: in the midst of my prose, which ranges from autobiographical to scholarly, you will find journal entries, dialogues, poetry, a letter, and sometimes drawings. As you encounter this somewhat unusually textured text which reflects my own expression, know that I intend it on one level to remind you to include the special manifestations of your own expressive gifts in y/our life-weaving. May we weave together richly polymorphic, many-colored tapestries!

My account of this process begins with the metaphor of weaving; chapter 1 explicates this metaphor in terms of my own search for self-knowledge and wholeness of life; I invite my readers to join me in a search we may all share to make life intentional, no matter what ways our Martha and Mary selves are like or different. I point to stories, ranging from autobiography to fairy tale, that illuminate this in-tending. I hope you will compare and contrast these stories with your own personal store of yarns, the shaping materials of your own life. All these strands may then be used to open a way to weave meditation of God, of God's love and guidance for each one of us, in and through the threads of daily life.

In chapter 2, I expand this discussion into fuller concentration upon the idea of how we may each proceed to weave our individual creative processes into alignment with God's Creation. There is an incarnational/divine principle of synergy possible in the weaving. Much as God, incarnate in Jesus, entered the lives of Mary and Martha, so our intentional life-weaving may invite His entering into ours. An analogue between our creating and God's unfolds in increasing awareness for us as we enter more and more deeply into the lifelong process of continuing conversion, of maturing faith. That is an underlying theme of this entire text-weaving; in this chapter I weave the anchoring strands of this analogue-web.

In the next chapter (3) I consider how we may commit ourselves to this creation/Creation analogue with others, within God's Household, within the loving, liberating context of God's hospitality. I find, with the aid of dialogues, wonderful flowerings of the concept of hospitality within the household of Martha and Mary with Jesus. The process of conversion is underway when Jesus is invited into the household, sharing hospitality. This process involves, as well, efforts to understand ''the one thing necessary.''

The household as image and metaphor helps me explore the idea that the ''way'' is one of service in the world based upon a loving, intimate relationship with God in Christ. We encounter God personally in the daily, mundane life of our own household; here we are ''grounded'' in the disciplined basis for our transformed vision. Our life in that personal household relationship with God then becomes the foundation for our participation in the larger community, in the all-embracing Household. I contrast this present-oriented partnership-modeling Household with what feels to me like a restricting future-oriented and dominance-modeling metaphor of Kingdom.

In chapter 4, I explore how we may encounter the knots of stereotyping in our weaving. I devote a whole chapter to this topic because at any point the conditions of being female and/or dominated by patriarchal hierarchies may sabotage our best efforts to give and receive hospitality in the Household. As I mentioned previously, I feel that our Western culture tends to give power to those who are "male Marthas," the doers who waste little time on reflection, on pursuits that qualify as "Marylike." We may find work we love, but find it closed to us because of our sex, or we may discover that we are not promoted or paid in our work as we would be if we were male. Particularly if we are women, but also if we are compassionate men in situations like these, we must meet the challenge of our anger, frustration, and sadness if our life-weaving or the life-weaving of our companions is not to be damaged or negated because of sexual stereotyping. Both our Martha and our Mary selves can be thwarted by stereotypes; hence, they are a threat to our wholeness.

Whereas I deal with this dilemma largely from a personal point of view in chapter 4, I present in chapter 5 the encouraging work of other scholars and artists who have found ways to imaginatively liberate the weaving from such oppressive limits. Beyond the conventional interpretations of women's and men's roles, beyond the conventional interpretations of the Mary and Martha stories, theological imagination sheds new Light.

"The Pattern of Discipleship: Threads of Mature Commitment," chapter 6, further considers the continuing process of maturing in faithful living within Scripture. I examine some of the language and scholarship surrounding the early Church practice of discipleship, and I study how Mary and Martha, each by a different path, find a way to wholeness in faith; there are illuminations for our own weaving here. I also discuss how we may deal affirmatively with our own anxieties as we continue weaving our own ways into discipleship—there are tensions to be balanced no matter how advanced we are as weavers.

In chapter 7, the final chapter of the text, I find that no matter what good way we have found to understand our own rhythms of solitude and community, of action and contemplation, in prayer we must learn to give up *our* control over the outcome of our service to God. It is as though we have finished an apprenticeship in discipleship, and we are now prepared to move skillfully into a new realm of the "disciplined/ spontaneous," of an apparently effortless flowing with the weaving itself. We move toward that weaving which is done *through* us, if we can so empty ourselves, by the incomprehensible mystery of God—an ideal weaving that paradoxically expresses all our unique skills as weavers-in-life *and* is part of the grand overarching web wherein we are blended into the centering radiance of God's glory. As we "see now through a glass darkly, but then face to face," so now we weave partially, but then fully into Light and Wholeness/Holiness. Though I establish the vision of an ideal here, I also discuss prayer as a way for us to dispel our illusions, to own up to our own pettiness and problems suffered even in the midst of well-meaning service from both our Martha and Mary selves, and to be comforted that God's glorious and caring love surrounds us.

As I write-weave this text, I consider us (writers/readers/ co-creators) to be in prayerful, continuing conversation. Together, we listen to God's Word in the text, and together we make our responses to this Word. Making these responses requires us to bring ourselves in our most wholeheartedly creative way into this work; this demands patience and honesty, and perhaps above all, *humility*. There is risk too: weaving is an ancient art related to initiation and rebirth. Once we undertake it, we are likely to find ourselves undergoing transformation; then there is no going back. But I feel encouraged for each one of us by the emphasis in these texts upon hospitality: we are both hosts and guests in this weaving, as you will see.

Chapter 1

Weaving: Why This Metaphor?
Making an Intentional Life Fabric

As the woven image/life experience grows, a work/person be-comes more whole. A successful weaving is like a person who knows herself (Kate Russell, 11).

Much as this work with Mary and Martha appeared in my life and demanded attention, so did the accompanying meta-phor of weaving. Though my practical experience with weav-ing has been quite ordinary—I have made simple potholders, mended holes in clothes and darned socks with a darning egg, plaited braids, wound Maypoles, and made woven paper-strip Easter baskets in school—I have always found it fascinating. I have several friends who weave on their own home looms and I love to wear the garments they have made.

As I thought of weaving in connection with Martha and Mary, I thought of a rhythmic, thoughtful process, repetitive but cumulative in constructing a fabric, a process that, under-taken with awareness of analogous Creation/creation, could provide a way to center upon God.

When I first began my weavings with the stories of Mary and Martha, I focused solely on Luke's brief scenario of them in their house with Jesus in chapter 10:38-42 (here and else-where I quote the RSV unless otherwise noted):

> Now as they went on their way, he entered a village; and a woman named Martha received him into her house. And she had a sister called Mary, who sat at the Lord's feet and listened to his teaching. But Martha was distracted with much serving; and she went to him and said, ''Lord, do you not care that my sister has left me to serve alone? Tell her then to help me.'' But the Lord answered her, ''Martha, Martha, you are anxious and troubled about many things; one thing is needful. Mary has chosen the good portion, which shall not be taken away from her.''

The conventional interpretations of the Martha and Mary story choose Mary over Martha; they elevate Mary for her quiet, prayerful attitude at Jesus' feet as they chastise Martha for her distracted busyness. With Martha as frenzied housewife and Mary as woman with no other calls upon her but contemplation, I felt neither one was an appropriate model for my life. I felt there were valuable lessons to learn from the stories of these two women, but I had to go beyond the usual interpretations to find them.

As I read and reflected upon these verses, I became so involved with them that for a while I forgot that there was a cluster of stories concerning the sisters in John. In John 11:1-44 the story centers on Martha's declaration of Jesus as the Christ and on Jesus' raising of Lazarus from the dead; in John 12:1-8, the story centers on Mary's anointing of Jesus' feet. I begin in this text as I began in my own encounter, with the verses from Luke, going on to the Johannine stories in later chapters.

The issues the Lukan story of Mary and Martha aroused for me were ones that snarled up into a skein of knots and confusions which I stubbornly believed could somehow be straightened and woven into something whole and even lovely. Surely we have all felt these insistent, emotional connections with sacred text; we read and know that we are being personally addressed. But we also know that the understandings we seek are not likely to be easy or immediate. We feel an urge to wait and weave together this text and our life, sensing that if we are faithful to the work, we shall receive a blessing.

In *FiberArts* magazine, another weaver, Kate Russell, writes about weaving in the way I had begun to consider it in relation to Martha, Mary, Jesus, and myself: "To me, weaving, with its moving threads, is a powerful metaphor for life. Thread meets thread in a weaving not unlike an individual moving through life, where each experience is the 'thread' building the 'fabric' of a lifetime. As the woven image/life experience grows, a work/person becomes more whole. A successful weaving is like a person that knows herself" (11).

The more I considered this project, the more I realized that weaving had become a basic metaphor not only here but in all my life work. One of the meanings of *work* is, in fact, *weaving*, from the Old English *wircan*. Erich Neumann in his book *The Great Mother: An Analysis of the Archetype* adds that " 'to weave' is the restricted form of 'to work' = 'to perform an opus' = 'to perform a sacred action' " (227, note).

Consciously weaving, we participate in a great universal mythic weaving/working. Diane Wolkstein, writing "Interpretations of Inanna's Stories and Hymns" (from ancient Sumer), provides this image: the Sumerian pictograph for *plant* is "two sets of four lines crossing each other at right angles forming a mesh, which is a third new entity, yet maintains the equal identities of the opposing forces" (144).

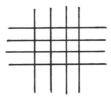

She suggests this pictograph displays wonderfully the synthesis of consciousness and unconsciousness, light and dark, male and female, the power of life and the power of death. In a similar way, I find this weaving/working functions for me as a great connecting with living Creation.

This Sumerian plant/mesh pictograph also makes me think of how incarnational weaving is. The loom is full of everything and nothing, a great potential until the warp is strung; still, the warp itself is merely lines of thread or string until the woof is interlaced: no one part is sufficient by itself. Warp and woof together work synergetically to create a whole that is more than the sum of its parts. I find that Jesus' dialogue with Martha and Mary is an affirmation of this incarnational/divine principle.

Weaving is conventionally defined (in an image mirroring that of the Sumerian *plant* pictograph) as "the interlacing of two sets of threads at right angles to each other so as to form a web of fabric." The two sets of threads in this Martha and Mary study are the biblical passages signifying holy Word which I use as warp, the foundation threads stretched taut lengthwise on the loom, and the materials I bring from my own life-researches (and which I encourage you to bring from yours) which are the weft threads (also called woof, filler, or simply weaving threads) which are laid through the warp threads, side to side or widthwise, in various ways to produce different types and patterns of cloth.

Sometimes I find the interlacing sets of threads to be voices, voices which weave back and forth in dialogues, sorting out the tensions and irregularities, the questions as well as the insights in the weaving. These dialogues form lines of color, motifs, and textures which are individual yet part of the universal Pattern.

I am considering here the belief in Pattern as faith; the creation of patterns in this context exemplifies for me "knowing now in part," a learning-in-process which some call continuing conversion. My way of participating in this process is to summon as many of my creative voices as possible in hopes that I can weave them and the varied parts of my life they represent into a wholeness. This is an organic process of which I write/weave. May it stimulate and companion your own.

The idea of life as a weaving, a weaving which is a learning-in-process, has been both comforting and instructive for me.

It reminds me to be patient; it reminds me to remain hopeful; it reminds me that each of us has the opportunity to enter with God into co-creation. Weaving is both active and contemplative, I believe, but never passive—it does not happen by itself. Although grace and guidance certainly enter in if we invite and wait upon them, we are called to live/weave our unique responses (that is, to exercise our response-ability).

Weaving and Rebirth

I have used the word "co-creation." By that I indicate my belief that, if we ask, God will be with us and will act with us in the weaving; also, that each of us is part of a community of weavers. Much as we are all members of one body and necessary each to each other for life and health (on every level), so as weavers we rely on each other's unique talents and offerings to make our fabric whole. The fact that some of us are more Mary-like or more Martha-like is only a beginning.

As weaving itself has a long, deep connection with the mysteries of co-creating, of initiation and rebirth, so the spirit of Jesus in this text may serve a spinster/midwife function (typically "feminine" functions which I hope my text may help re-authenticate). If we draw upon ancient traditions, we may see Jesus' attendance upon our rebirthing within the matrix of mysteries once presided over by the Great Goddess:

> The thread motif, which incorporates the idea of spinning, weaving and a complexity of beliefs in the knot as an instrument of magic and the weaving of spells, runs throughout the tradition of the mythology of rebirth and its attendant artifacts; whatever form it takes, it is always associated with the realm of the Feminine. The motif survives even in the fairy tales of Europe in which the themes of spinning and weaving are frequently encountered. There are as many variations on the symbolic thread device as there are names of goddesses, and what is described in many of the myths are rites of initiation that facilitate the passages from one stage of life, or consciousness, to the next, over which the Goddess, or an emblem of her, presides as "mistress of initiation" (Johnson and Boyd 64).

As I weave and begin to be transformed in the weaving, I realize how much I rely upon a marvelous network of persons who have shared their unique talents with me. Two essential muses of the work are Lorna Shoemaker, whose article "Martha and Mary: A Study in Wholeness" gave me the idea for this study, and Mary Daly, whose writing inspired me to develop the metaphor of weaving.

In her work, Daly lent me Seraphic Spinsters, encouraging Weaver Angels. I call on these Angels as I weave. They give wings to this sometimes heavy work; they help me to keep discipline and delight in balance as I go. They also hold me to a larger perspective: I have been called to weave awhile on this Mary-Martha theme because it challenges me to name myself and my work; it challenges me to perceive my own and others' "women's work" transformed. The Angels, sitting on the four corners of the loom, gently insist I keep in mind that naming is holy work—it is the healing-wholing stuff of the Household of God. "Remember," I hear them say, "while you will have plenty of tough lessons to learn in this weaving, this is, above all, Light work!"

The Miller's Daughter Spins Straw Into Gold

There have been times when I argued with my Weaver Angels: Why have you commissioned me to write-weave about this particular story? Why did it choose me? What business did I have to choose it and then announce publicly that I would carry through with weaving it? Heaven knows there have been times when I've felt as forlorn as the young woman sitting in the room of straw she has to spin into gold, before the appearance of the strange little man, Rumpelstiltskin.

Like the miller's daughter, I feel thrust into the spinning. She is forced to it by her father's prideful lie to the king that she can spin straw into gold; I am compelled to it because of the dualistic lie of sexual, hierarchical stereotyping and because my own internalization of its fragmenting "disempowerment" is something I vow to overcome. Both the daughter and I act "as if" we can do what we don't yet know how to do. We receive help, but we both must meet this challenge through faith: what has at one point "saved" us, given us protective cover (for her the tiny man, for me a less-clear amalgam of role choices according to a patriarchal society's norms), now threatens to take our child, the fruits of our creativity, if we remain enslaved to it.

Once we *name* Rumpelstiltskin or our own unintegrated weaver self, we *ourselves* can weave the gold of our own lives. I understand that process to be one I cannot complete alone; I must do my best to go as far as I can in naming myself and finding my life, but there is the paradox then of "losing to find," a mystery that I must trust Christ and the Holy Spirit to weave with me.

In her essay "Straw and Gold: Consciousness and the Mature Woman," Helen Luke asks, "How do we spin the straw of our lives into gold? Fundamentally it is a matter of a glimpse, a momentary, intuitive glimpse at this stage, of the ultimate truth beyond the opposites, that straw and gold are one thing" (73). Luke emphasizes the accidental nature of the miller's daughter's discovering Rumpelstiltskin's name; for her it exemplifies our need to do everything in our power to be "awake enough to hear the name when it is spoken. . . . The real goal of all our efforts is to arrive at the capacity for this goal-less waiting" (78). Our gift then is the "safety of the 'child,' the new possibility of wholeness in the mother" (Luke, 78).

Other times I feel a kind of ecstasy as everything suddenly seems to belong in this fabric; I wish I could say mystically, "Everything is everything"—it's all interrelated far more than we can imagine and is therefore ineffable, absurd to even try articulating—and leave it at that. But again and again I return to the work because others have believed in it and I do, too. I have faith that this wrestling of fibers in the loom will yield its own as-yet-unknown pattern, its own as-yet-unknown gifts.

Some Weaving Word Roots

I am learning as I weave to trust that the Light weaves us as we weave it, and all according to our birth-gifts, our experiences, our peculiar individual enthusiasms (*en-theos*—our own "in-God" fascinations, allurements). I am a reader, a writer, a teacher, and a lover of texts, among other things, so I am naturally intrigued by word-roots. There are several key ones in this weaving.

The first is the Latin root *texere* which means "to weave." In reminding me that this is also the common root for both "text" and "textile," Mary Daly provides me with a major pattern in *Gyn/Ecology: The Metaethics of Radical Feminism* (4–5). In many ways I have identified myself as a person pressured by the uneven tensions of these two worlds of text and textile, as scholar-teacher and as housewife-mother. In the Mary-Martha story, I sense an opportunity to unweave the badly begun web of what I believe is an essentially false duality and to reweave it into a unity. Thinking of the work "context," I imagine a way in which I may learn to see "within the text" which combines both "text" and "textile"; I will learn how to see them together, a blending like the two interlocking teardrop shapes of a classic Chinese yin-yang symbol. But this will be no easy blending, no easy weave-over, for Mary has long been identified with the world of text as Martha has long been identified with the world of textile, and they have often been viewed as separate realities (especially by me!).

So for me, and quite possibly for you, too, this is a story which "looms up" and demands to be woven-with. Even before I have come to this point of sitting down to spin-script, I have already woven and un-woven numerous strips of biding-time, pondering, yet-unripe work. But even this pre-weaving unweaving is part of the process of beginning to order. Daly reminds me that this is no haphazard order I intend; it is Creative Ordering suggested by the Latin word *ordiri*, meaning to lay the warp, begin to weave, begin . . . (Daly, *Pure Lust*, 292). Only how and where to begin?

Journaling as Weaving: Preparation for Dialogues

My own beginning was in journaling, Elena Malits' suggestion. Mary Daly's etymological discussion of *texere* as the root of text and textile made me realize that this story of Mary and Martha had a history (herstory!) for me. I asked myself, as I encourage you to ask yourself: "How am I Martha?" "How am I Mary?" "How have my temperament, my background, my education, my relationships, my general life-experiences, attitudes, and aspirations shaped the Mary-and-Martha-ness that I am (or am not)?"

As I pondered such questions, I began to write out dialogues—between the sisters, between the sisters and Jesus, between the sisters and Jesus and myself. I tried to understand my dissatisfaction with previous interpretations I had heard or read about the Luke passage. I questioned how I was meeting obstacles that kept arising to prevent this. I asked myself what particular supports I had or needed to help me make right choices. Were the supports I wished to create or maintain ones of persons, of disciplines, of particular environments and attitudes or . . . ? I asked how my private and public works might be seen more integrally related not only to each other, but to the larger context of the Household of God.

I asked myself if my own personal responses related to cultural and social norms and how I felt about my answers. And as I wrote, weaving the dialogues and thoughts into the fabric of my journal, I discovered that these questions were multifaceted and truly central to me. This "little" story began to grow—it was as though I'd begun with the thought of weaving a potholder and had been overtaken with the urge to create a tapestry.

As I share some of my own dialogues, I hope that you will be writing your own. I know that mine are individual, but I offer them in the hope that they will companion and encourage yours. I suggest that sometimes you intersperse your writing with drawing. I have occasionally taken out oil pastels or just the pen I was currently using and tried to draw my response to the scripture. I thought about just how I would symbolize Mary and Martha and their complementarity; I found myself thinking about their hands—what do they hold and what attitude do they assume as I imagine them? I imagined colors too;

which ones would you assign to the sisters together and singly?

Again, I remember weaver Kate Russell's words: ''I compare my work to life: a life, like a woven fabric, can be deconstructed and then re-formed through an understanding of its structure'' (11). As I wrote in my journal, parts of this structure emerged.

I grew up in what I would call a very ''Martha'' household. My dad came from a big Pennsylvania farm family. His dad had necessarily instilled in his children the virtue of hard work. When my sisters and I grumbled out of bed after my dad called to wake us up for school, he would occasionally remind us that for him, as a boy, at eight o'clock the morning would be half over, milking having begun around four or four-thirty. Mother and Daddy kept our household, and our car and farm equipment business as well, on a busy, productive course. As the family ''bookworm,'' I quickly learned that there was a difference between visible work that ''counted'' and invisible work (I barely called it ''work,'' this solitary reading and thinking, writing and drawing) that had less ''countability.'' I became a competent houseworker—ironing, cooking, sewing, and cleaning (I was the stereotypical conscientious eldest child). But I learned rather bitterly that housework often didn't ''show'' the way I wanted it to since it constantly had to be redone. Sometimes I felt like leaving all the dishes out and the ironing hanging on hooks outside the closets so that all this repetitive and quickly undone work would be visible.

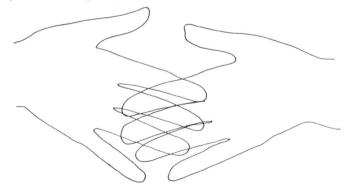

This is not to say that reading or writing were discouraged. My parents actively supported our schoolwork achievement; they read to us, bought us encyclopedias, made many books and magazines available, and took us to the lending library in town. I remember, for example, reading many of the "classics" from a set Daddy won by selling lots of Champion spark plugs. It was just that I saw that these activities came *after* the "real work" and that the only way I could validate myself in pursuing them was to bring home high grades from school and to avoid, at all costs, being lazy about housework (laziness was second only to lying as a cardinal sin in our household). In terms of this weaving, I found my Martha self, the one active at "textile" or domestic work, easy to affirm; the Mary self, this quiet, scholarly, and "text"-oriented self, though encouraged in her own way, was somehow secondary.

As I have said, my difficulties with what I perceived to be a Mary-Martha dichotomy stemmed from the known and appreciated practicality of my Martha abilities and the unknown fragility (and tenuous marketability) of my Mary pursuits. I was very close to making a choice to major in home economics at the state university, but a scholarship to a Church-related liberal arts college led me instead to study literature and humanities. Something mysterious and rather confusing called me to develop this Mary self even though I wasn't sure just how and where she belonged in the world.

I am embarrassed to say how long it has taken me to come to accept both my Mary and Martha selves. My assumption of the cultural bias toward them as polarities too long divided me against myself. I trusted my practical Martha self but could not en-spirit her; I committed myself to develop my Mary self but could not fully trust or empower her. That is how it seems to me now. I believe that I am brought to weave this story on my loom in order to see at last that I am not hopelessly fractured but on a graced journey toward wholeness. And I offer these weavings in the hope that you will join me on this journey.

Not too long ago I had a revealing conversation with an old

friend. We were both saying what drudges we'd been in college and graduate school, and how we wished that we had gone out and had a good time more often. While we were lamenting these poor, over-worked Martha selves, we suddenly had the insight that without the foundations they had laid for us, we would not have the options for both our Mary and our Martha selves that we have today. Our Marthas' hard work was necessary for us to get our education and our degree-credentializing so that we could go on into ministry (for her) and teaching (for me) which utilized not only our Marthas but also our Marys, both in ways impossible without that early Martha work. We had awakened wiser selves within us that were able to heartily thank our young Martha selves for their diligence. In this instance we recognized how we needed to be involved in the continuing work of reconciliation/weaving of Martha and Mary. My suspicion is that this is true for many of us.

Here is a further definition of *weave*, from the *Oxford English Dictionary*: "1. intr. To move repeatedly from side to side; to toss *to and fro*; to sway the body alternately to one side and the other; to pursue a devious course, thread one's way amid obstructions." These definitions seem to include a sense of game, of dance, along with elements of mystery and chance and definite risk.

"To thread one's way amid obstructions"—indeed. I have no illusions about this weaving-writing resolving all the conflicts I somehow attached to in my growing-up time. I have vulnerabilities and biases I will have to take into consideration during my entire lifetime weaving; unless I am vigilant, they can block the work of Spirit. One of the ways I have discovered which helps me understand my underlying structure is to toss ideas to and fro in dialogue. Though I usually conceive of the dialoguing voices as two internal aspects of my own self, that is only one way to consider them; I hope that you will experiment with ways in which they inspire your own internal and external dialogues.

The first way I began to work with these dialogues was to

assign independent status to the parts of me I've called my Mary and Martha selves. So you will see in the following dialogue that when I am letting Martha and Mary speak they are parts of my total self. Though they are based on the New Testament figures, I have projected the qualities I imagine them to have into my own life situation. Thus I am using journaling as a way of exploring my own values, my own faith journey. In the dialogues I consider how these women and their roles in the New Testament witness may clarify questions which daily life raises for me and for others. This technique of journaling with Scripture is not one I have invented, but I hope that my particular use of it may be useful.

Dialogues

In my journal the (Nancy)Mary-(Nancy)Martha dialogues begin:

> Mary: Why do you have to be like that? And don't ask me "Like what?" You know—trying to embarrass me in front of Jesus.
>
> Martha: I *wasn't* trying to embarrass you. I simply felt we'd all get to eat sooner if you'd give me some help. Do you think you're the only one who wants to sit at his feet?
>
> Mary: I look at you and I think, "Oh yes, she's being productive; she's doing things and being admired, whereas I feel suspect somehow in this action-oriented culture." It's so easy for me to feel I'm not pulling my fair share of the load. Even in retreat and study times where I feel my intellectual and contemplative selves being encouraged to blossom, it is sometimes hard for me to feel confident that this is what I should be doing [note the *should* here!]. I am growing less insecure about this, but traces of my old reticences linger.
>
> I really felt my vulnerabilities when I called home once when I was away for study and learned that the sink in

my daughter's bathroom had to be replaced, that our refrigerator had stopped working, and that my husband was having to tend to all this alone. Even though I knew that I often gave him support for his work, I felt terrible and somehow wrong not to be there. That's when I realized I had to stop myself from taking all the blame, assuming all the guilt. I saw it was high time I stopped doubting I deserved equal time and not just leftover time when the "real" work had been finished and I was exhausted anyway. I could be thankful for our mutually supporting each other and free to not be guilt-stopped when it was my turn.

Martha: I get so tired of your whining about being unappreciated. Hell, Mary, I yell at you, but I *need* you. Won't you please be *you* even when I don't have enough sense to know that's what *I* as well as you need! I can't carry all this burden of doing and doing without your being alive and well. I know our work-ethic culture admires me (you remember how much I inwardly preened when anybody like Grammy or Daddy said solicitously, "Don't work so hard, dear!" We both knew they meant, "How wonderful that you work so hard; you really represent our family values well, but we don't want you to overdo." When they said that, I always took it as an occasion to be both proud and self-pitying—poor me, how hard I work and how little I am really appreciated).

But Mary, it's only when you are doing your work (I use that word consciously) of prayer and contemplation, of being at Jesus' feet, that I can carry on my work without that perverse pride and self-pity. You connect me with "the one thing needful," and that makes the difference between my being a harried housewife or, rather, a woman who understands the implications of her work. You help me know that I am working in the Household of God. You help change my greed for "productivity" into a desire for fruitfulness of both body and spirit.

Mary: You mustn't speak too quickly of how you are resolving all these tricky questions of the different modes of being we represent. It's taking me a good while to learn what I'm really about. If I fulfill the need for contemplation, for prayer, even for poetry in us, I can tell you right away that I'm not always certain how to live that out. You seem so self-assured and confident of *your* way; you know what you want and how to get it. I, on the other hand, often feel wordlessly needy—the ''word person'' left paradoxically wordless. Sometimes I feel myself nearly suffocating in knowing things too inwardly, too personally, too intimately, and fearing that who I am and what I do does not relate responsibly to the larger world. I fear that I have learned things I must share, but am not confident enough to do this effectively. But I know I must acknowledge that and pray for help in connecting us.

What keeps me going is this one fact: I know I need to be at Jesus' feet now and so I am. I feel loved and fed in his presence. I really do feel like a weaker, younger sister next to your powerful, articulate, and bustling self, but I admit this and look for guidance in clarity about my purpose.

Martha: You're right, Mary, that I seldom lack words, and I have great motivation and skill to actively serve, but these too must be brought back again and again to God. For me, the great temptation is to be a nag and a judge—I see what is to be done and I feel others should join me. I have trouble sorting out what is only mine to do and what I should bring, prophetically, to the attention of the community. It's hard for me to keep priorities straight—I can so easily be overwhelmed by unsorted business.

Mary: I'm ashamed to admit it, but I often hide behind your unsorted priority frenzies. In a kind of self-pitying lassitude I stand by and willingly martyr myself to your crowded agendas. You seem to know what you are doing, but I'm not sure I can develop my tentative projects, so I lose heart. Yet, I know my special task is the discipline of listening, of paying attention to the gifts of the Spirit which are mine. I need you, Martha, for all you do in the community, for your skill in working ideas out into action, and I am gaining the courage to tell you forthrightly that you need me for the balance I provide to your busyness in my quiet contemplation at Jesus' feet.

In a slightly different mood, the dialogue included this exchange:

Mary: I know I am hungry, but I don't know the right questions to ask to be fed; do you know?

Martha: Maybe. But when I want to be fed, I get up and fix a meal. It's simple. I know how to do that, and I do it well. So here I am again, doing what I know how to do and *can* do and I'm doing it because it's needed. You don't think you can be fed *only* on Jesus' words do you?

Mary: No. I am fairly certain of my "daily bread" in the physical material sense, and I thank you for providing me with it. But Jesus' food feeds my greatest hunger. I need to be near him. It doesn't even matter so much *what* he says as *how* he says it and what his radiance means in my life.

Martha: Yes, I believe I understand that, but part of what I want to warn you about is this: you can't be "at his feet" in that physical way all your life even if you *are* being metaphysically fed. You have to get up and *do* something.

Mary: You may be right, Martha, but I have to be obstinate about this for now [Mary even means "obstinate" in some etymologies!], and maybe obstinacy is what I need in order to wait long enough in his presence until I am sure how to proceed.

On Solitude and Community

As an affirmation of the preceding dialogue section and as an amplification of it, I quote a section from Parker Palmer's *To Know as We are Known: A Spirituality of Education;* clearly, the dichotomy between solitude and community he discusses is not exactly the same as that between contemplation and action which I've been using as a general distinction between Mary and Martha, but it is an extension of the idea of their mutuality:

> Solitude opens us to the heart of love which makes community possible; life in community manifests the love we touch in solitude. Community requires solitude to renew its bonds; solitude requires community to express and test these bonds. If we live at one or the other pole of the paradox, we sacrifice either the inward content or the outward form of truth itself (122).

This weaving, then, is to forever be a delicate balancing of tensions, those of action and contemplation, of solitude and community, of the inner and the outer. In my meditation-weaving I discover that all these many-dimensional aspects of my Mary and Martha selves have legitimate and life-enhancing claims for expression. How shall I adjust the loom, my life, so that I can weave them harmoniously, synergetically together? My Weaver Angels whisper to me that I must pray as I weave the great disciples' prayer, the prayer that triumphantly ends the *Revelation* of John: "Come, Lord Jesus," or in Aramaic, "Maranatha." Then I will weave rightly, in the way I alone can weave in his presence. Then and then only will I be able to weave these selves together peacefully.

> Martha: What gives me great joy, Mary, despite our different strengths and weaknesses, is that we have received Jesus into our house. With him here, I feel we will learn how we complement and complete each other, how he brings us into wholeness. In a way, I trade my serving the food for your listening at his feet today; an-

other day you may serve and I may listen; or I will learn fully to listen *as* I serve and you will know how to serve as you listen or even *by* your listening.

It's very hard to know just how this will happen, but I know it will happen as long as our heart-hearth is open to him.

A real breakthrough for my determination in this weaving came when I was ordained as an elder in the Presbyterian Church. I felt I no longer had the choice of fuddling around in dualities. I needed to assume fully for myself *and for others* the powers of wholeness I had been, for all kinds of reasons, denying. I could not act childishly. I no longer had, I felt, any right to withhold the "all of me" I knew was needed for the task. I had to trust that this wholeness would somehow emerge in conjunction with power supremely beyond me: God in the person of Jesus, the Christ-shuttle in my weaving metaphor. It quickly became apparent that even though I saw that many of the designated tasks I would undertake as an elder were Martha work, I could never do this without the constant strengthening and guidance of the Mary work of prayer and contemplation. It is as though I received an ordination-commission for this weaving.

Chapter 2

Weaving and Creative Process: Aligning Our Individual Lives with Creation

Thou it was who didst fashion my inward parts; thou didst knit me together in my mother's womb (Ps 139:13).

If there is a joyous, loving center to our faith and to the universe, as I believe there is, how may we live *in touch* with it? If I were to name what boon I wish to take from this study project, it would be to learn how to do just that. The corollary would be to learn how to *let go* of everything that keeps me from that loving joy. I don't want to mope and mutter; I want to sing and dance!

The Mary and Martha stories were clearly given to me as a challenge: Can you learn ways to reconcile the opposites you have felt them representing in your life, Nancy? And can you weave/write the path of your learning in such a way that shows you are learning how, even as you go, to use both your Martha and your Mary selves? Since you are a writer/teacher, use the stories to model for yourself and others the rich new possibilities for writing, teaching, and living that a harmonically interacting Martha and Mary with Jesus might demonstrate. Can you keep in fruitful interaction your Mary link with prayer and contemplation and your Martha link with skillful action? Above all, can you make this a creative process marked by joy, by an attitude of openness to all that may come, giving thanks as you go?

Thus I intend this chapter as a "situating," an "orienting" which in weaving terms is analogous to dedicating one's best material, best skill, and best heart, if you will, to the project about to begin. This preparation, which precedes the first actual work, the "dressing" of the loom, is full of prayerful hope. I do it so carefully because I know that this particular project can never be finished unless I have guidance obtainable only through prayer and a listening to Wisdom beyond my own. I intuit as I begin that I will be meeting some of my own "gumption traps," to use a term from Robert M. Pirsig, and that some of them are really mucky. Martha and Mary do not have a good relationship within my history, and I have much conflict to face and to resolve if we are to end as cooperative sister weavers. Hence, I cannot overemphasize how important this stage of individual preparation is for the work ahead.

Again, I put forth this individual experience in my life to suggest general principles. I believe that any individual work, no matter how particularly dedicated to be shared publicly, must still be wrestled with until the creator finds a "fit," a placing of the work within a matrix integrating body, mind, and spirit. This allows it to become luminous in a way that enables the person who initiates it to give it the fullest attention and creative energy.

In asking myself how to dress this loom—to set it up, make it straight and true, align it from the beginning—I tried to envision an interpenetration of Mary and Martha threads on the loom weft. As I thought of who Martha and Mary were to me, I saw that I would have to settle issues I had somehow muddled into by accepting a mess of stereotypes; I had dualized through Martha and Mary not only the qualities of action vs. contemplation, but the areas of the public/secular vs. those of the private/sacred. How can I make this a truly worshipful creative project? How can I enlarge my definition of worship to include what I normally consider "secular" with what I normally consider "sacred"? How will I bring my own individual fears and flaws into understanding that can lift up not just me but also others? How will I enter what seems like a labyrinth without becoming desperately lost in the darknesses and confusions I am sure I will encounter along my path toward Light? In short, how will I engage in this project in the most responsible, Spirit-directed way and bring it to completion?

The same questions must be asked of the many projects that each one of us may be engaged in: How can we do our creative work, which is often Martha-like, without being distracted, with a deep and harmonic connection with our Mary selves? Have we made time and place for the work, and have we a community within which our work and our worship are acknowledged as one? How do we place all our weaving/working in the context of "the one thing necessary"?

An Aligning Image: Mother Mary's Loom

One answer to these questions came in the form of an image, a gift of one of my Coolidge Colloquium friends, Carol Purtle. In some fifteenth-century Flemish devotional paintings there is a panel underneath the principal imagery, a kind of thematic foundation; in it Mother Mary weaves on a simple loom stretched between two poles. As she knits on her womb-loom the breath-threads of Spirit into incarnate Word, so I feel God helps us weave Spirit into our own writing-wefting, breathing-being; then, and then only, may our creations reflect Creation. (For examples of this image, see Carol Purtle's *The Marian Paintings of Jan Van Eyck*, Plates 5 and 6, from the Boucicault master and workshop—two annunciations, each from a Book of Hours.)

In this image, Mary is the daughter of an age-old lineage of weaver women. Erich Neumann writes that "It is not by accident that we speak of the body's 'tissues,' for the tissue woven by the Feminine in the cosmos and in the uterus of woman is life and destiny" (*Great Mother*, 227). ("Tissue" is another connective word root in this study: it is based on the Old French *tissu*, past participle of *tistre*, "to weave," which stems from the Latin *texere*!)

Boucicaut Master, Annunciation, Florence, Corsini Collection (Book of Hours), *The Marian Paintings of Jan Van Eyck*, Plate 5.

In the Protevangelium of James, a non-canonical gospel which gives an account of the birth and dedication of Mary as well as of the birth of her son Jesus, we find another reference to Mary's weaving. According to this text, after Joseph was miraculously chosen as her husband in the Temple when she was twelve, a council of priests resolved to make a veil for the Temple. They found seven pure virgins of the tribe of David, including Mary. When they were assembled, the priest said, "Cast me lots, who shall weave the gold, the amiant, the linen, the silk, the hyacinth-blue, the scarlet and the pure purple" (10.2). Mary's lot was to weave the "pure purple" and the "scarlet."

In a highly symbolic sequence, Mary began to spin the scarlet, the color of blood. When she took a pitcher (an ancient and enduring symbol of the feminine) to draw water, she heard the voice of the angel of annunciation: "And trembling she went to her house and put down the pitcher and took the purple [the color of royalty] and sat down on her seat and drew out (the thread)" (11.1). In words familiar to us from the first chapter of Luke, the angel told her she would bear "the Son of the Highest," and she humbly assented.

After preparing the purple and scarlet portion of the veil, Mary took it to the priest; he blessed her and her work, saying, "Mary, the Lord God has magnified your name, and you shall be blessed among all generations of the earth" (12.1).

Commenting upon this non-canonical gospel story, Gareth Knight writes that the veil spinning and weaving continues the tradition of the Fates of the pre-Olympian myths and the weaving of the Veil of Isis, "the veil of phenomenal appearance that cloaks inner reality" (152). He notes that Mary's weaving of the purple and scarlet portion of the veil is blessed as is the weaving of the purple and scarlet of "the lineaments of the god man [which] are to be woven within her womb" (154).

We can see that the Mary/Spinster image weaves from the ancient Mothering mysteries into the Fathering/Mothering mysteries of Jewish and Christian traditions. From these images in the paintings and in the Protevangelium of James, I turn to the music of Psalm 139 which they call forth for me:

> Whither shall I go from thy Spirit? Or whither shall I flee from thy presence?
> . . . For thou didst form my inward parts, thou didst knit me together in my mother's womb. I praise thee, for thou art fearful and wonderful. Wonderful are thy works! (139:7,13–14)

May the image of Mary weaving and this psalm both undergird this weaving.

A Loom Dressing Dialogue

If only I could always hold myself in the Light of this image and psalm. But this weaving is intimately connected with my life, and I am anxious about dressing the loom, about beginning. I wrote about this in dialogue form, again allowing myself to hear imaginatively the voices of the Martha-Nancy and the Mary-Nancy selves who argued within me at the time I first considered this writing:

> Martha: Yes, I see you want me to work with you on this, to lend all my active, aggressive, in-the-world skills, but something tells me that this weaving is really *your* "thing."
>
> Mary: Well, Martha, I will take major responsibility for initiating this project, and I see that it's hard for both of us. When we began this work, all we had was a kind of sense that this weaving on our life-looms was "numinous," i.e., it had a light around it—a Light, we learned!—that drew us toward it. When we got to the Coolidge Colloquium for a month of work along with twenty-four others, you remember how afraid we were that this work we'd tentatively outlined was too small, too constricted and narrowed down to ever become anything? We felt that everyone else there was admirably studying the edifice of the Universe and we had stupidly concentrated on just one brick.

Martha: And it was the kind of work that seemed to have to come out of the Unknown in an organic way that neither of us could predict. That's what really unnerved me. I felt torn away from familiar places and routines (I had left my home and family in sunny St. Petersburg to fly up to live in a dorm with a group of strangers in chilly Boston); I missed making meals and doing washes and weeding in the garden; I wanted to talk with my husband and daughter. I missed, as I always do at the end of semesters, my students as well as my colleague-friends and our collaborations. In short, I longed to be distracted from this imponderable project.

Mary: I know that, and I love your courage in persevering with me. You dared to enter with me into the kind of disciplined silence and waiting I knew we had to hold ourselves in if this weaving was to come into existence.

Martha: And I was surprised (and delighted) to see that it *did*! I learned a great deal about how we cooperate in the creative process. I tell you, Mary, I felt it as a double affirmation—you needed me and I needed you, and we worked together in a way we never really did before. I believe your insistence upon daily centering in meditation and in yoga as well as in community worship at the Colloquium opened our collaboration to Spirit in a wonderful new way.

I also saw in condensed time the necessary creative cycle you've often linked with the Greek story of Persephone and Demeter, of descent and fallow time before ascent and growth time. It was as though we came here wishing it was already time to burst out into new growth and to go straight into flowering and fruiting when we had barely begun the descent. We had to allow for this time before beginning to form the unformed. We had to allow for this time before we could emerge into the time of action-fruition, the time when I can finally come into my own. I'm really amazed that we were able to do this.

Mary: Although I usually understand such periods of gestation in terms of mythic symbols, one of my friends suggested to me that they had analogues in the lore of science also. I found a marvelous passage from *The Auto-biography of Nathaniel Southgate Shaler* as demonstration. What I see in it is another example of how the relatively mundane can reveal a world (note *mundus*, or "world" in Latin as root of mundane!) *if* we attend to it with persistence and discernment.

In this passage, the young Shaler begins work in the laboratory under the tutelage of the famous Louis Agassiz. Agassiz brings him a small fish in a tin pan with the requirement that he study it without talking to anyone else and without reading anything related to it without permission. When Shaler thinks he's finished with his assigned task of learning all he can without damaging the specimen, Agassiz ignores him. Recognizing the situation as a game of wits, he goes further—"in the course of a hundred hours or so [I] thought I had done much—a hundred times as much as seemed possible at the start." At the end of the seventh day of study, Agassiz asks Shaler what he's learned; when Shaler finishes with his report, he's told "That is not right" and is left once more alone with the fish. Taking this as a challenge to his ability to do "hard, continuous work without the support of a teacher," Shaler writes "I went at the task anew, discarded my first notes, and in another week of ten hours a day labor I had results which astonished myself and satisfied him" (6).

I admit to as much astonishment in the results of *our* persistence as Shaler professes to have had with his own. And it interests me very much to find that what we did was so like this scientific process.

Martha: Another metaphor I'd add: in the Colloquium situation it was as though we were given our own alchemical vessel. Within a simple framework of morning worship, of shared weekday meals, we carried out our individual projects, the main scholarly work of the Colloquium. In the local libraries and our own rooms we hermetically sealed ourselves and cooked until our *prima materia* was transformed. Only then did we have a seed we could finally plant and tend and trust for golden fruiting (forgive my mixing metaphors, but I hope you see what I mean).

Mary: Oh, yes, but be careful not to say we "earned" this or "worked hard to deserve it"—your proclivity, dear sister—but to note that what happened was very much a grace we "put ourselves in the way of." We were invited into "sacred space" and given precious time to focus intently upon our work. We even had friends and colleagues to help us notice it, celebrate it, and begin to form it for sharing!

The Spirit of Play in Our Aligning

As I dress or arrange and order this loom which is my life for this particular weaving, I ask, what kind of loom is it? Sometimes I imagine it as a horizontal frame loom, sometimes a two-bar vertical Navajo loom hung between poles out of doors in the bright desert sunlight. In any case I connect my loom with all looms, all lives. I loved discovering this link with my community of weavers through all time. Probably the earliest evidence of the use of a loom has been found in a woman's tomb at Al Badari in central Egypt, the date ca. 4400 B.C.E. In a wonderful coincidence of feminine images, a bowl found there is decorated with a representation of a horizontal loom ("Weaving," *Encyclopaedia Britannica*).

In dressing the loom I ask these imagining questions in order to keep the place where I work as much a "playshop" as a workshop. The Mary and Martha weaving connects with the core of my effort to learn how to live an integrated life. This story touches upon deep places of wounding; in dealing with it, I am forced to acknowledge great needs for forgiveness and healing. I myself am the keeper of the often destructive dualities possible between Mary and Martha. At the same time, this weaving is showing me the joyous healing potential in a Mary and Martha unity.

All this, I hope, raises questions for you about your own unique needs to nurture a sound, alive bodymindspirit. What is your own creative style? How do you keep tuned? Are there parts of you longing for better nourishment, fuller exercise? How can you arrange your life to make this possible? (Here, I must acknowledge the incredibly free space I have in the academic life for such arranging; I have grateful humility about that. You may have much less freedom, but still there is a basic question of priority—each of us must choose what is our own way to focus on "the one thing necessary.") Again, I encourage you to reflect upon this in journaling; or you might, given your own particular ways to open and listen, dance or draw or sculpt or otherwise express your visions of wholeness in bodymindspirit. Ask yourself if this exploration is best done alone; you might, at various points of your journey, wish to gather or join a group. You might need to alter your ways of worship; you might consider finding a spiritual director, if you do not have one, to help you find your way and to companion you upon it.

One of my friends says she must meditate and dance before writing if her work is to be true. Another begins her day by praying over the telephone with a partner. Another relies upon an international network of friends who give each other "wake-up" calls each day; in these brief calls, they help each other focus upon the work they do individually but understand within community.

Another important part of the loom-dressing for me is building in some ways to avoid my temptation to become over-serious and heavy with "oughts" in such work. I have understood that this spin-scripting is not to be a drudgery; that would be an affront to the Spirit who inspires it. Yet I persist in all sorts of self-pitying, envying, fearing, anxiety-mongering heaviness. I have dialogued enough with my Mary and Martha selves to know that both are vulnerable to becoming drudges—Martha in her kitchen and Mary in her study.

My Buddhist sisters have taught me about creative play that the witty, iconoclastic feminine spirits called *dakinis*, or "skywalkers," inspire. The "dakini principle" involves being able to shift out of a "stuck place" and into new life. This is what I believe Martha does after Jesus' gentle rebuke. In Buddhist stories, the dakini often appears when a nun or monk becomes inflexible or arrogant in discipline. For example, the dakini might bring to one whose vegetarianism has become idolatrous a plate of freshly butchered flesh. If the person rejects this gift and the opportunity for growth it represents, the spiritual way itself is blocked for that individual. We might apply the "dakini principle" to Martha's story: Jesus asks her to "smash the idol" of her overly assiduous and self-martyring service in order to grow.

Two Models: Quiché Weaving and Jewish Midrash

At times when I am bogged down, I search for words, for images, for keys in any form to open again the way to Light. In one such time (and forgive me if I have not adequately acknowledged these frequent "gumption-trapped" times; they humble me into remembrance that conversion is continuing and requires community), an image like the Mary-loom came as a gift. It was in an article another of my Coolidge friends suggested, "Text and Textile: Language and Technology in the Arts of the Quiché Maya," by Barbara and Dennis Tedlock. I loved this passage the moment I read it:

> Among the contemporary Quiché weavers, textile designs are considered to be ancient, which makes their continuing use something like the quotation of an ancient text. The ideal context for the work of weaving calls for words in the form of a running conversation, and the best place is a spot in a cornfield. In her autobiography, Rigoberta Menchu describes the situation as follows: "There's a place in the fields which is so wonderful and pretty and shady that all the girls get together—7

or 8 of us—and sit under the trees and hang up our weaving. We talk and weave'' (126).

What a sparkling, life-filled picture! I welcome its opening the work up to sunlight and growth and laughter and friendship. I imagine fireflies and moonlight weaving the cornfields at night, birds and butterflies, sunlight and shadows weaving them by day, the girls weaving in an in-and-out dance as they thread the shuttles back and forth in the looms hung amid the singing green-blue-gold world.

The Tedlocks write that ''among the contemporary Quiché Maya of Guatemala, there are intertextualities within and among such arts as instrumental music, storytelling, prayer-making, dream interpretation, divination, weaving, house-building, and horticulture'' (123). This kind of interdisciplinary intertextuality (I believe the Quiché Maya would call it simply *life* and I am inclined to agree) excites and inspires me. How can we bring this much life, this much radiant beauty to our understanding of Mary and Martha? In fact, how may we so imbue *all* our life-looming?

The ways in which the Quiché weavers use the ancient designs, like the quotation of an ancient text, seem very much to me like Jewish midrash—a weaving of stories, of other texts, of life experiences and insights in and around sacred text. Whenever I have had the pleasure of ''doing midrash'' with Jewish colleagues, I have been delighted at the mood of profoundly serious playfulness that prevails. There is the reading of the sacred text, the recounting of rabbinic commentaries and folk stories surrounding it; then there is the bringing of one's own special life knowledge to bear, to give witness to the ''living Torah,'' the text as it illuminates our time and place. People so engaged truly know themselves to be weaving sacred space together, like a great tent or prayer shawl over and around all.

As the midrash and the Quiché weaving model so beautifully, sacred text is to be reverenced with the *all* of our lives. And it is done, quite consciously, within the context, through space and time, of the community.

In the midrash and the Quiché weaving I also feel lifted by the poetry of language and of visual images. They are an invitation to write our own poems, to paint our own pictures, to dance and sing and weave and otherwise architect our responses to sacred text. I find myself writing poems, writing journal entries, drawing, and sometimes dancing in response; although this is solitary expression, I feel in it the ongoing strength and inspiration of community.

The Luke text begins: "Jesus entered a village; and a woman named Martha received him into her house." I ask myself, "How can I invite Jesus into *my* house, how can I bring *all* of my life into God's presence?" If you are like me, you have kept certain portions of yourself sealed away from your weaving. You have hidden caches of yarn, skeins you hoard. You have compartmentalized your life and made choices about which compartments are open in which situations; not even in God's presence are they all open.

I recollect a time when I was on retreat, a kind of "defenses down" time when I allowed myself to peek into my "sealed away" compartments. I was alone in a wintry field, sitting on a bale of hay when I heard a voice saying to me "God wants *all* of you." At that moment I understood that parts of me I generally call "erotic, artistic, and radical," were part of the being God loved and invited *me* to love and to express. Though I had seldom found invitations to engage in the arts, to literally dance, to be myself as powerful womanbodymindspirit in the Protestant traditions, I heard then a permission-giving command to find ways to express my wholeness. This weaving, then, is a beginning for the task I have set myself of learning to gather the "all of me" in myself and others.

Another time, during a journaling workshop (another place and space like open fields and green forests in which I find myself more-than-usually open to honest listening), the woman who led it made a statement I carry with me like a talisman: "There is no human experience outside the realm of God's grace." At these moments I began to admit which parts of me I was holding back from integrity within myself and within my community; I resolved to bring as much as I could of my *all* into my life-looming.

Ann and Barry Ulanov's *Primary Speech: A Psychology of Prayer* has helped me see further how to bring my *all* into God's presence:

> Prayer is willingness. We will not be given more if we refuse what has already been given to us. We cannot expect anything to be added or changed in us if we are not willing to accept the facts about us and especially those facts, hidden away from everybody else, that only we know. . . . Thus our way to God, to discovering that God is already there with us, can only proceed in the flesh and through its passions, through our fullest humanity, what Christ promised as the abundant life (10, 12).

The Word Roots of "Line" and "Linen"

Let me use one more weaving metaphor to illuminate this process of preparation. I have mentioned how much it means for me to be able periodically to have time to savor solitude in the beauty and relative quiet of nature; these times literally "ground" me. So, in the spirit of "playshop" I enjoy the "grounding" of another Latin word root in this weaving: the common root cluster of *line, linea, Linus* which branches out to both *line* (written) and *linen* (woven). Flax is of the genus *Linum*; the Latin root flowers blue-blossomed into the mother of both *linen* and *linseed*. It bursts out in lines on bookleaves; the linseed is often used in making the paints and printing inks with which the lined leaves are illumined. (I intuit a wide-branched lineage that includes the Sumerian pictograph of plant/woven mesh!)

I find linen mentioned more than any other cloth in the Bible. In the Old Testament, in Exodus and Leviticus, it is established as the material to be used for the garments of Aaron and the priests—an ephod (a kind of apron), a robe, a coat, a turban, and a girdle, all were to be made of fine linen and gold, blue, purple, and scarlet "stuff," skillfully worked (see Exodus 28:3-9). In Leviticus 16:32 we find the description of the ritual of atonement: "And the priest who is anointed and consecrated as priest in his father's place shall make atonement, wearing the holy linen garments.''

In the Gospels, linen is mentioned mostly as Jesus' burial cloth. John 19:40: ''They took the body of Jesus, and bound it in linen cloths with the spices, as is the burial custom of the Jews.'' Linen was the material in which Lazarus was wrapped for burial as well. In the *Revelation* of John (15:6), angels are ''robed in pure bright linen''; the Bride of the Lamb was granted '' 'to be clothed with fine linen, bright and pure'—for the fine linen is the righteous deeds of the saints'' (19:8); and ''the armies of heaven, arrayed in fine linen, white and pure'' follow the one called Faithful and True who sits upon the white horse (19:14, 11).

Linen seems scripturally to be the fabric of holiness—of ritual celebration, of suffering and death, and finally triumph. In using this fiber as our thread, we weave into our lives, symbolically and materially, the sacred. Though this tracing of linen-lines may seem a bit stretched, still it becomes a thought-thread to connect us with our faith lineage.

I think of Jesus' words of acclaim for Mary: ''Mary has chosen the good portion, which shall not be taken away from her.'' I believe that both Mary's and Martha's lives, as our own, once we make a faith commitment, are dedicated to learning how to live out this choice. What does it mean to live out this intentional choice of ''the good portion'' in the daily in-and-out weaving of our lives with sacred text, our mundane intertwining with these holy linen-lines we seek to clothe ourselves in?

Using linen, the most ancient of textile fibers, predating even cotton, we connect with eons of flowering-fruiting earth, the tradition of weavers as far back as the Stone Age. In the Minoan period of Crete, writes Charlene Spretnak in *Lost Goddesses of Early Greece*, pre-Hellenic Athena ''nurtured all the arts, but Her favorites were weaving and pottery'' (99). The Goddess appeared to women working in a field and ''broke open the stems of blue-flowered flax and showed them how the threadlike fibers could be spun and then woven'' (100).

As we weave our life-weavings with the Mary-Martha scrip-
tures or any others, we compare the durability of linen and
the fact that years of constant use bleaches hand-woven linens
to a snowy whiteness with our attentive Scripture weaving-
meditating. There is a sense, too, in which this return to the
beginnings of this weaving art reminds us of the Beginning
of all Being. I think of the first two verses of the Gospel of John:
"In the beginning was the Word, and the Word was with God;
and the Word was God. He was in the beginning with God;
all things were made through him, and without him was not
anything made that was made." The Word is essential, "origin-
all" warp; Christ as incarnation is for Martha and Mary and
each one of us the Friend/Spinster who encourages us to weave
the radiant warp and weft of the Household together.

Chapter 3

Weaving Relationship with Others: Household and Hospitality

Perhaps all artists were, in a sense, housewives: tenders of the earth household. Perhaps a nurturing sensibility had never been more needed (Erica Jong, 119).

In the process I am recording here, of learning how to reconcile Martha and Mary in myself and my world within the presence of Jesus, the all-encompassing Word, I turn from concerns which must be settled individually to ones which open out explicitly into community. Since the stories of Martha and Mary in the New Testament witness so deeply to Jesus' companionship to each of us as persons, it seemed entirely right that we use the metaphor of household. I choose this definitely over metaphors like "kingdom" which suggest a dominance-submission relationship, a set of hierarchies within which persons must demonstrate blind obedience to authority. What fills me with joy and hope as I study with Martha, Mary, and Jesus, is the sense that I am included in an intimate household where each of us extends as we are able the fullest sense of hospitality to each other and to each other's gifts.

We return to the beginning of the Luke text (10:38-42): "Jesus entered a village; and a woman named Martha received him into her house.'' Martha has dressed the loom, has assumed actively the responsibility as weaver of her life and has taken the initiative to invite Jesus to be present in her household, her loom, her life-weaving. This receiving of Jesus is not to be taken lightly; it is a hospitality that others, particularly the Samaritans of the village cited in Luke 9:53, have denied him "because his face was set toward Jerusalem," i.e., they refused to aid "pilgrims going to keep a feast at what they regarded as the wrong sanctuary" (see Oxford RSV note, 1258). If we connect this text with the text of John 4:19-27 in which Jesus speaks of "true worship" with the woman of Samaria drawing water at the well, we note that first Martha and then her sister Mary understand the true spirit of worship and of sanctuary which Jesus is redefining. In the John passage, the woman refers to the Samaritans' holy mountain (Mount Gerizim, where they had had a temple, Oxford RSV note, 1289), but Jesus says: "Woman, believe me, the hour is coming when neither on this mountain nor in Jerusalem will you worship the Father. . . . the hour is coming, and now is, when the true worshippers will worship the Father in spirit and truth, for such the Father seeks to worship him. God is spirit, and those who worship him must worship in spirit and truth" (4:21, 23–24).

In Luke 10, which ends with the Mary and Martha story, the initial verses tell of the mission of the seventy; they are commissioned to go and teach the good news. If they are received in a village they are told to "eat what is set before you; heal the sick in it and say to them, 'The kingdom of God has come near to you'" (10:8-9). Otherwise, if they are rejected, they are to shake the dust of the town from their feet and remind the villagers that a judgment falls upon them. These disciples experience great joy in their work, a joy which Jesus experiences in the Holy Spirit in gratitude. He tells the disciples privately that they are blessed to see what they see: "For I tell you that many prophets and kings desired to see what you see, and did not see it, and to hear what you hear, and did not hear it" (10:24).

When we bring these events and these sayings of Jesus to bear upon the humble scene at the home of Mary and Martha, it seems that Jesus acknowledges that these women, especially Mary in this incident, have seen and heard what the disciples have been graced to see and hear and are thus included among them. Furthermore, in conjunction with the re-definition of worship and sanctuary which Jesus teaches (and which he personifies), they understand that worship and sanctuary are indeed matters of the spirit: where Jesus is invited and honored, worship occurs; where he is invited to be present, sanctuary is. It is as though this episode ''grounds'' the teaching of this section in an intimate domestic setting. Where Christ is received as friend and teacher, there household (loom) becomes sanctuary and what occurs in his presence—living/working/weaving—is worship.

In these passages, Jesus presents Mary and Martha and each one of us with a central paradox of his being: he is present with each one of us in our own household when we invite him in; he is at the same time master of the universal Household, present to all who acknowledge him. Not only that, but he shows us that none may say he is present only at ''special'' sanctified sites at ''special'' sanctified times—he IS for us in time and space when and where we ''worship him in spirit and truth.'' I believe there is a corollary too, that his power is never an abstraction, never only a glorious Platonic reality. He personifies a power of presence that mysteriously interweaves the mundane world of our households with a great Household in which he invites us to live with him. And the ''grounding'' of such a deceptively domestic story as that of Jesus' visit with Martha and Mary shows us that we cannot forego the daily tasks of common life in order to become holy; they are the foundation of our living faith.

The more I study ecology and consider it in terms of the ''the earth household'' (a term which I first learned from the poets Erica Jong and Gary Snyder), the more powerful I believe this metaphor is for us as individuals and as community. It reminds us of how much we depend upon great webs of interconnections between our lives and those of all members of the ''earth household.'' In terms of Christ's presence, we learn that this Household embraces all realms of household-ing and challenges us to live in ways that interweave them into a holy wholeness.

Oikos: The Greek Word for ''House''

The word Luke uses for ''house'' in 10:38 is the Greek *oikian* (or, elsewhere, *oikos*). In Greek the related word from the same root, *oikoumenikos*, refers to ''the whole world''; the word *oikoumene* is ''the inhabited world,'' from *oikein*, ''to inhabit.'' Our word ''economy'' stems from the Greek *oikonomos* ''manager of a household''; our word ''ecology'' stems from the Greek *oikos*, ''house'' plus *logos* meaning ''study''; our word ''ecumenical'' again refers to the Greek words cited which refer to the whole or inhabited world (cf. etymology in *The American Heritage Dictionary of the English Language* 1976). Especially when read in connection with Paul's great use of the metaphor of the household in Ephesians 2, it seems right to discuss this story of Jesus, Martha, and Mary as suggestive of all the households connected in One: ''So then you are no longer strangers and sojourners, but you are fellow citizens with the saints and members of the household [*oikeioi*] of God, built upon the foundation of the apostles and prophets, Christ Jesus himself being the cornerstone, in whom the whole structure is joined together and grows into a holy temple in the Lord; in whom you also are built into it for a dwelling place of God in the Spirit'' (Ephesians 2:19-22).

We must enter the humble house of Martha and Mary with Jesus and base our lives faithfully there in order to enter the glorious Household of God. This seems one of the central les-sons of this ''way'' we learn when we weave these stories with our own. Jesus said, ''In my father's house are many man-sions;'' we might think of the mansions as the separate house-holds which together form the ''father's house.'' Since a priest friend of mine told me that the "mansions" were way stations for soldiers along the Appian Way, I have thought it appropriate to consider that our households too represent "way" stations for the pilgrimages of all who come to share our hospitality. As we grow in our own pilgrimage, our own faith journey, we too must enter different mansions/households, knowing always that we are sojourners. Thus we are led to understand that our households are places for renewal, for worship, for daily life; they are places along the way wherein we place ourselves under the tutelage of the Holy Spirit. She shows us how to allow the Household of God to interweave, daily and more fully, with our own households.

The words we now use which are rooted in the Greek for house/household remind us that in our household we are connected through ecology, economy, and ecumenism with all others. The "one thing necessary" understood in its fullest terms provides the center for all the concentric household-worlds, and provides a guide by which we may manage our households, aligning their material dimensions with the spiritual, understanding them always as parts of a Whole. Isn't it extraordinary how many conventional boundaries, stereotypes, and limits become meaningless in this Light?

This acknowledgment of household/Household connection can provide a radical shift in our attitude toward life. When our weaving brings us to this point of new vision, it is as though we have entered a new household, a new "way." Entering this or any new household entails crossing thresholds, a symbolic act, like weaving, which has to do with transformation. It strikes me that as Martha welcomes Jesus across her threshold, she herself symbolically crosses a threshold. In the pattern of the hero's or heroine's journey as defined by Joseph Campbell in his studies (see *The Hero of a 1,000 Faces*, for example), the crossing of the threshold indicates the departure from an established known place and entry into an unknown realm. Inviting Jesus into her home, Martha risks transformation for herself and those who dwell with her (Mary in the Lukan passage; Lazarus also in the Johannine passages).

The Reciprocity of Hospitality

Martha offers hospitality to Jesus; it seems she does not quite realize the full reciprocity of that hospitality which Jesus offers her. In Luke 12:37 Jesus says: "Blessed are those servants whom the master finds awake when he comes; truly, I say to you, he will gird himself and have them sit at table, and he will come and serve them." In hospitality we do indeed open ourselves to risk, to the presence of a guest who may have been a stranger but now, at least briefly, is included in the intimate circle of the household. It is true that the guest may overstay his or her welcome, drink too much and bore or insult the other guests or the hosts, break a glass or steal the silverware; it is also true that the guest may become a lasting friend, may offer words of encouragement, may bring healing and life-changing good news. Jesus was this latter kind of guest, one who confounded Martha and who confounds us with his own hospitality when we offer ours.

The reciprocity of hospitality which I am discussing is found in the Latin root, *hospitare*, which means both "to receive as guest" and "to be a guest." Further derivations of this root in English and French connect "host," "guest," and "stranger" as well. In a *Sojourners* interview, Gordon Cosby, founder of the Church of the Savior in Washington, D.C., defines spirituality with the image of "intimacy in a relationship with Jesus" (16). It seems to me that the household of Martha and Mary exemplifies the hospitality which is both reciprocal and intimate in significant ways. What Martha must learn is that she must give up her need to keep the host-guest relationship static; Jesus exemplifies the dynamic of host-guesting and commends Mary's understanding of it in this instance. Martha appropriately acts as host when she invites Jesus into her household and goes about serving him. She has to be reminded, though, that Jesus' presence brings her household into the infinite reaches of his Household, in which he offers her his hosting and she needs to gracefully accept her role as guest. This understanding of host and guest is truly a radical one. (Later, in chapter 4, I weave further on this theme as it relates to the master-servant relationship.)

I have spoken of what I perceive to be a meaning of Martha's inviting Jesus across her threshold into her home; as I pondered this, I realized that in studying these texts I also have crossed a threshold and invited a crossing. This crossing marks entrance into a realm of new knowledge and experience. In crossing the threshold of Scripture, we are invited to interact and weave with it as part of our growth in faith. Any text which calls us to it may become this entryway; in my case the Mary and Martha stories have been an allurement which has led me into scriptural study and meditation. This small brick has led me to connections with the greater edifice. Furthermore, I realized that at first the "greater edifice" was just too overwhelming; it was forbiddingly abstract and "out of my field" until these stories gave me a personal connection, a special motivation which seemed intimate and hospitable to my entering.

Having resolved not to be a life-long threshold sitter, I believe I can make this statement of what I learned as I encountered the threshold of this study-writing-weaving: "If you are called to cross a threshold, and if you believe it will eventually lead to Light, ask the Spirit to go with you and do not neglect to cross over."

Seeking the "One Thing Necessary"

Martha has bravely invited Jesus into her household; her crossing of this threshold opens her to life-changing lessons. To see how these unfold, for her and for us, we continue with the text of Luke 10:39-42: "And she had a sister called Mary, who sat at the Lord's feet and listened to his teaching. But Martha was distracted with much serving; and she went to him and said, 'Lord, do you not care that my sister has left me to serve alone? Tell her then to help me.' But the Lord answered her, 'Martha, Martha, you are anxious and troubled about many things; one thing is needful. Mary has chosen the good portion, which shall not be taken away from her.' ''

The climax of the text, Jesus' response to Martha's irritated request in verses 41 and 42, is beset by textual problems. Of the six identified variations, two have the strongest scholarly support. The longer of the two preferred readings focuses on the meal setting: "Martha, you are anxious and troubled about many things; *few things are needful or one.*" One commentator suggests the meaning could be: "A couple of olives, or even one, will suffice at present. Mary has the main course already." The shorter and more widely accepted version (as quoted from the RSV above) is, "Martha, you are anxious and troubled about many things: *one thing is needful.*" The latter is in keeping with other passages in Luke: Jesus' words to the rich young man (18:22) that *"One* thing you still lack"; the woman with ten drachmas who will sweep out her house in search of "one" (15:8); and Jesus' words, "No *one* is good but God alone" (18:19). (For full discussion of these textual variants, see Aelred Baker's "One Thing Necessary.")

Using the interpretative principle stated by Rabbi Akiba, "Every section in Scripture is explained by the one that stands next to it," we note that the passage is directly preceded by the parable of the Good Samaritan and followed by an account of Jesus' teaching the disciples how to pray. I turn first to the passages preceding Martha and Mary's story (I turn later, in chapter 5, to the passage following it, of Jesus' teaching of prayer).

In his commentary, Charles H. Talbert finds that the whole of 10:29-42 is Luke's exposition of the two great love commandments of 10:27. What is most useful to me in his discussion is the suggestion that the Good Samaritan story may function either as a catalyst for conversion as it shatters stereotypes or as a confirmation for those already converted; it appears that the Mary-Martha story may be similarly double-functioning. But his conclusion disturbs me: "To love one's neighbor means to act like the Samaritan. To love God means to act like Mary" (126).

In this conclusion, I am reminded of how so many interpretations of this passage simply reinforce dualities the two sisters may represent. As I read this I hear a too-common message: the Mary-Martha text-textile dichotomies so uneasily balanced in myself are doomed to be fixed and inevitable. Martha is, in this conventional pattern of interpretation, the person stuck in works righteousness; she exemplifies what many women in the Church have felt—that they perform the tedious, menial tasks so necessary to its functioning, but are somehow left feeling worthless.

Martha in Dialogue with Jesus

I feel such empathy for her frustration. As I write, Martha's voice threads onto the loom in prayer:

> In this stewpot of a world
> I intend to brew nourishment;
> why rebuke me for furiously feeding
> even you? even yours?
>
> Oh Lord—in my Martha heart
> love breaks forth, a clamor
> of pots and pans, of claims and causes,
> insisting, insisting that I serve.
>
> I would be quiet if I could
> but I seem called to bake and weave;
> I would be shamed to leave you
> naked and hungry as you teach!
>
> Distracted though I can be
> my heart bends to your words—
> what more is this you ask of me?

(Nancy Corson Carter, in *Womenpsalms* [Winona, Minn.: St. Mary's Press, 1992])

Martha speaks for me, for all of us distracted by the very nature of our vocation—how much energy it takes to do what we see needs doing and know that we can do. And if we mean well by it (and we do!), how much more shameful to suddenly be made to realize that our well-meaning is so off-center. Martha might, as I might, since the temptation is very present, retreat in anger, but she does not. I imaginatively elaborate the text here, assuming that if Martha has invited Jesus across the threshold of her home, she has committed herself to learning what lessons she may in his presence.

I write another dialogue in my journal, this time between Martha and Jesus:

> Martha: Jesus, you know, your reply to my asking you to get Mary to help me really made me angry. I thought to myself, "Here he is, our guest, and I am troubling myself to make him a nice meal. Instead of being appreciative, he's telling me I'm overdoing it and missing what's important besides. The nerve!" When I cooled down a bit, I could begin to understand what you meant, but I still worried whether you were teaching me as a friend or as "just a woman," though I haven't felt you doing that ever before. Still, your admonishing me about what is mostly "women's work" made me feel the burden of women's inferior status in our culture.
>
> Jesus: Martha, I hear you. I would not admonish you if I didn't trust your ability to discern my meaning. You and your sister and brother are my beloved friends [ed. note: I connect the Johannine information about their brother Lazarus with Luke's story although he mentions neither Lazarus nor their living in Bethany as John does]. I make this statement about the one thing needful in your household not to demean women or "women's work" or the mundane world of housekeeping in any way, but to point out that the one thing needful is or *can be* fully present in this context. I love you in your activity, Martha, as I love Mary in her contemplation. I simply wish for you

not to be anxious about any false hierarchies of persons or talents or needs. Let Mary nourish herself as she needs; let yourself be nourished also.

I need your food, Martha, as you need mine; let us in hospitality exchange these foods with humility and with patience. Let this eating and this serving be hallowed by awareness of God, our source. When you hold yourself in this awareness, you are God's priest serving Eucharist.

So I keep imagining and learning as the weaving proceeds. I too often find myself needing to swallow pride and get on with learning the lessons I am shamefully confronted by; I keep having to learn and re-learn forgiveness, especially for *me*, for my own stumbling, bumbling, anxiety-ridden processes, for the ways in which I myself am responsible for nasty tangles in the work.

Seeking to Honor Unique Gifts

As I read and study and meditate, I become more and more certain that Jesus brought to earth in his ministry a revisioning of what it means to be *person*, fully human woman or man, so radical that even his disciples, both the women and the men, were pushed to their limits in allowing its enactment. He insisted, as he does here in the scene with Martha and Mary, that each person be allowed to fulfill her or his own vocation without the stultifying barriers of sexuality, class, culture, or race. It was a vision of incredible allure, but also of great threat to those unused to such freedom.

Jesus' vision of what it means to be fully human entails enormous responsibility; it is a responsibility to undertake the painful, long-term process of becoming a mature human being, one who knows, by disciplined and loving attention to God, what her or his own vocation is, and who dares to enact that vocation within the Household of God.

Reading Elisabeth Schüssler Fiorenza's *In Memory of Her: A Feminist Theological Reconstruction of Christian Origins* has caused me to consider carefully my use of the term "Household of God." Since the household in her terms becomes a rigid patriarchal institution, she chooses the word *ekklesia*, which she defines in the New Testament context as "the actual assembly of free citizens gathering for deciding their own spiritual-political affairs."

I must insist, however, on the term "Household of God" because of its significance to my theme: Jesus enters into our most intimate, most basic structure of life-relationships and there invites us to enter into a conversion experience which aligns our "household" macrocosmically with his Household. As human beings we cannot escape living in households; whatever happens in the church or *ekklesia* is based upon that foundational social structure. In the microcosmic household, we encounter all the prejudices and hierarchies which threaten our wholeness; we invite Jesus' presence there to help us, in love, to burst the shackles of convention.

This is a radical challenge to our way of being, and it is crucial if we are to bring the parts of our lives ordinarily polarized as private-public or secular-sacred into congruence. Once engaged in this re-visioning of householding, we are to help each other form a complete, interdependent staff of householders; if each person develops her own unique abilities and uses them to the common good in an attitude of grateful reverence, will not this be the Household? Yet it is easy to see in this story as well as in our own lives just how difficult this is to achieve.

Martha doesn't speak directly to Mary; she speaks to Jesus as a whining child would complain to her parent about the misdeeds of a sibling. The way in which she complains is not quite direct, not quite honest. No doubt she deserved some help, but she seems to be asking not just for help but for some kind of value judgment against Mary from Jesus. His reply was obviously an upsetting one to her. Somehow I am reminded of the numerous occasions in which I have been preparing a meal while others are watching TV or reading or doing "their own things,'' and I feel the rankling resentment of being ''put upon''; I have plenty of experience to feel wronged along with Martha by Jesus' rebuke. Yet, I keep asking myself: ''What is the lesson here? Surely not a mere rebuking of 'women's work'?!''

I am reminded of Talbert's insight that the whole of Luke 10:29-42 is the gospel writer's exposition of the two great love commandments of 10:27: ''You shall love the Lord your God with all your heart, and with all your soul, and with all your strength, and with all your mind; and your neighbor as yourself.''

Mary sits at the feet of Jesus and listens to his teaching. Being ''at the feet of Jesus'' as Paul claimed he had been ''at the feet of Gamaliel'' in Acts 22:3 meant in the language of the rabbis that she was a disciple. Jesus' encouragement of Mary's vocation of the intellectual, contemplative life ran counter to the orthodox belief that formal learning, such as skills of reading and writing, belonged only to men. In this story as in others, notably Luke 11:27-28 when the woman calls out, ''Blessed is the womb that bore you and the breasts that you sucked!'' and Jesus replies, ''Blessed rather are those who hear the word of God and keep it!'', according to Arthur Frederick Ide in *The Teachings of Jesus on Women*, Jesus affirms that women are *persons* in the eyes of God before they are babymakers or standard housekeepers.

Still, the rebuke is in no way aimed at Martha's housekeeping role per se, I believe, but is aimed instead at her apparent inability in this situation to ''love Mary as herself,'' to allow both her sister and herself to pursue their own vocations with loving patience. Rosemary Haughton suggests that in this story we ''catch a glimpse of what might be called Martha's conversion'' (85). If Martha had, as older sister, carefully trained Mary in her woman's role, then it may have come as a complete shock to realize Mary's choice of this unorthodox role, a woman disciple of the Rabbi, and furthermore, to realize that Jesus knew and approved. Jesus was challenging Martha, writes Haughton, ''to recognize a demand that over-rode the demands of her woman's world." She found herself propelled beyond the well-defended security of her own household by a power that called her, in Haughton's words, "to be vulnerable, not in control, drifting on a raft driven by the unpredictable wind of the Spirit" (86).

It is as though Jesus gives Martha the freedom to *choose* her own life, not changing it very much, perhaps, in outward form, but transforming it entirely in its inward spirit. Something momentous happens between the time of the account Luke gives us of the two sisters and the time of the account in John when Martha makes a great confession of faith, "You are the Christ," when Jesus arrives at their home after Lazarus' death. When I meditate upon my own experience of continuing conversion in relation to the Martha and Mary stories, I know that I, too, have well-defended resistances against becoming vulnerable to the motion of Spirit.

We might ask ourselves (as an extension of the question I posed in the previous chapter, "What am I holding back from God in my life?") if we are in any way like Martha, defending parts of us that keep us imprisoned even though they are essentially of good intent. Sometimes I am led to uncover these defenses in my life when I become jealous of someone else's life. Not too long ago I wrote an entry in my journal about the issue of *living my own life*:

> It's such an idolatry that I have allowed myself to practice: imagining that others' lives are so much more fun, fruitful, and virtuous than mine. I take an asset, that is, my ability to recognize in others their gifts and contributions, and then I pervert it—I let myself take this affirmative recognition and use it for self-deprecation. What a stupid, life-denying habit to invest so much energy in! Martha's peevish complaint to Jesus about Mary can, from one perspective, be understood as exactly this: she doesn't want to take responsibility for her own life, its peculiar gifts and tasks. Like me, she too quickly assumes that Mary is being more fruitful, more favored, and she unconsciously wants to sidetrack her as she has already

sidetracked herself by failing to recognize that her own life task is important. From this off-center point of view, she insists that Mary "stop her life" and be something other than what she at that moment truly is.

I think too of Martha's not addressing Mary directly but through Jesus. It is, perhaps, as if we pray to God to straighten out a fight or to have help in our lives while at the same time we ignore what practical steps we might take. I am reminded to speak directly to those with whom I have a quarrel or from whom I need help. Otherwise, I am trying to use God as a "Big Daddy" whose word I can then childishly convey to those whom I wish to coerce to my tasks—"You have to because Daddy said so!"

I have a lot of responsibility-shouldering to do in terms of this issue. There are so many ways in which I let myself be hooked away from freely giving, freely enjoying my own life and its tasks. I tend to watch families larger than my own and feel that I "should" have had more children or I should have produced more tangible "products" like books or photographs or courses, like "other people." (Do you hear the same petulant echoes I hear, of children cajoling their parents with declarations that "everybody else" is doing this or having that?) I tend to watch people (like my husband) who read and write much more rapidly than I do and become infuriated with my own slowness; I tend to watch people I admire who are busier than I deem myself to be, at work I consider "better" than my own and let my admiration be subverted into jealousy and self-deprecation. I name these "hooks" because I know we all have them in some form or other, and I know for myself just how much they can sap the joy of life.

So my challenge, like Martha's, is to accept others' lives and especially to accept my own. I write out this prayer:

> God, I have this flaw of vision; I name it before you and I repent of it. I know some of what it has cost— that it has made me blind to the gifts you so abundantly pour

out upon my life, those gifts of my own abilities and insights and work, those gifts of my precious family and friends, those particular gifts that fill each of my hours *if only I will hold them up to you*; it has made me too often unable to rejoice in the special gifts of others' lives. Let me be so filled with your Spirit that I let these logs flow away from my eyes; then my heart will be flooded with the radiance with which you have always surrounded me. I ask this in Christ's name, Amen.

In the hospitality-sharing we experience if we invite Jesus into our household, we learn what radiance, what warmth he brings. He becomes our hearth/heart and teaches us, *if* we will undertake the attentive keeping of this compassionate flame; in this way we are joined to the hearth/heart of the Universal Household. In this way, all our gifts become food of the hearth/heart which abundantly feeds each of us.

Hospitality as embodied in Jesus is the heart of our household. He comes to us as a stranger who makes us feel ''at home'' as we have never felt before (even in our own households!). He invites us to ''Lighten'' our tasks with the understanding that we, too, are sojourners. Nevertheless, as member/sojourners of ''the earth household'' we may be the joyous, compassionate host/guests he *encourages* us (literally, ''gives us heart'') to be.

Chapter 4

Is This Weaving "Only Women's Work"? Untangling Knots of Stereotyping

> *The limitation of women to the realm of "distaff" has mutilated and condensed our Divine Right of creative weaving to the darning of socks* (Mary Daly, *Gyn/Ecology*, 5).
>
> *"That our love for each other's work give us love for one another.*
> *That our love for each other give us love for each other's work"* (From Denise Levertov's "Prayer for Revolutionary Love," 97).

Up until this point, I have been weaving around the question this chapter poses; now I want to address it directly. When I ask in the title, "Is This Weaving 'Only Women's Work' "? the word "only" is ambiguous; it could be construed to mean a derogatory "only" (i.e., something easily dismissed) or an exclusive "only" (i.e., for women only—and perhaps still derogatory). It is this exclusive "only" which I mean to address. During the time I have been weaving along with Martha and Mary, I have grown to understand this work as belonging to both men and women; but I have had to begin with issues revolving around the fact of my being a woman responding to a text involving two other women along with Jesus.

When I feel I am, like Martha and Mary in their home, *alone* with Jesus, I have no qualms about being accepted fully as person—I have never felt that Jesus in any way thought of a derogatory category called "women's work." It is only when I step into the street outside that I realize how much enslavement exists for women and men in my patriarchal society (and, unfortunately, how much I have internalized this). When I address the issues of action and contemplation for persons like myself, I realize that gender issues impinge in ways that must be recognized.

If, as my own particular biographical details and dialogues indicate, I have difficulty in appropriating the strengths of both my Mary and Martha selves and seeing them whole, I would be greatly helped, I believe, to find models of such yearned-for wholeness. To be born a woman in a patriarchal culture makes this a difficult task. But then, it follows that it is a difficult task for men as well, because patriarchy by its very nature involves imprisoning stereotypes to identify and reward "proper" sex and gender roles in its hierarchy.

If we happen to fit the stereotypes, the outward signs of "fitting in," as Martha did, then we are in danger of solidification, of a smug and "distracted" preoccupation with wholly acceptable and "successful" work; we are also less likely to be compassionate and understanding with those who don't fit the stereotypes than with those who do (especially if we cannot assume a safe, condescendingly "virtuous" or "good" attitude toward them, but instead feel threatened by their unconventionality). If, like Mary, we trespass the "proper" boundaries of stereotypical vocation, we have difficulty in affirming ourselves, in finding a solid foundation for a work which doesn't fit the acceptable criteria of success and worth.

This raises a whole series of questions for each of us—how well do we fit the stereotypical sex and gender roles in our culture? How compassionate are we toward others whose vocations draw them into uncomfortably unorthodox places in the society? How understanding and forgiving are we toward ourselves and others when we find ourselves unable to be accepting of some "deviation"? And by what standards, if we are to override the cultural norms, are we to affirm and to celebrate our own and others' unique wholeness? I am assuming a wholeness which Jesus refers to as a life centered in "the one thing necessary." I am assuming that "the one thing necessary" may, as we yield to the Spirit's guidance, take us into uncharted places, places in the weaving where the pattern appears only as we dare to keep weaving and have faith that it *will* appear wholly (and possibly not in our own lifetimes!).

I must acknowledge my own privilege in this culture: I "fit in" with the North American dominant culture racially, ethnically, and in religious background—a WASP; the primary elements of my "misfit" are in my sex and in my vocation. I understand that the difficulties I experience might be excruciatingly intensified if I were "misfit" in several other categories.

Who Are My Sister Weavers?

Part of my own effort to "deconstruct and re-form" my life has been to seek help from feminist artists and writers. Mary Daly, as I have previously noted, is one who has deeply inspired me. Her feisty iconoclasm challenges me to cease clinging to weakening habits of thought and action. "Spinster," she writes, is a word of deception implanted in our language; rather than a term of deprecation as it is commonly used, its deep meaning is "a woman whose occupation is to spin" (Daly, *Gyn/Ecology*, 3). "There is no reason to limit the meaning of this rich and cosmic verb. A woman whose occupation is to spin participates in the whirling movement of creation. She who has chosen her Self, who defines her Self, by choice, neither in relation to children nor to men, who is Self-identified, is a Spinster, a whirling dervish, spinning in a new time/space" (3–4). In regard to the text-textile split, she writes:

> The limitation of women to the realm of "distaff" has mutilated and condensed our Divine Right of creative weaving to the darning of socks. . . . Small wonder that many women feel repug-

nance for the realm of the distaff, which has literally been the sweatshop and prison of female bodies and spirits. Small wonder that many women have seen the male kingdom of texts as an appealing escape from the tomb-town of textiles which has symbolized the confinement/reduction of female energy. The kingdom of male-authored texts has appeared to be the ideal realm to be reached/entered, for we have been educated to forget that professional "knowledge" is our stolen process (5).

Daly begins the introduction to *Gyn/Ecology* with an epigraph from Helen Diner's *Mothers and Amazons*: "All mother goddesses spin and weave. . . . Everything that is comes out of them: They weave the world tapestry out of genesis and demise, 'threads appearing and disappearing rhythmically' " (1). For me, this quote is a reminder of the great connections between Divine Creativity and human making that fully embrace the female; it serves as an inspiration for all the reconstructing and re-forming that I must do in my life because I was born female in a male-dominant culture. It also reminds me of the great birth-death dimensions of the weaving each one of us creates in a lifetime.

When I began to explore the women weavers I have known, I found I had a marvelously rich matrix for this Martha-Mary-Jesus weaving. I remembered figures like the Fates, Penelope, and Arachne from Greek lore and Spider Woman in southwestern American Indian myths. Barbara Walker, in *The Woman's Encyclopedia of Myths and Secrets*, expands my list:

> In Greek myth the three Fates were Horae, Graeae, Muses, Gorgons, Furies, and other trinities as well as the principal trinity of Moerae or Fates. The Moerae were Clotho the Spinner, Lachesis the Measurer, and Atropos the Cutter of life's thread. Nearly always the Fates were weavers. In Anglo-Saxon literature, fate is "woven." Latin *destino* (destiny) means that which is woven, or fixed with cords and threads; fate is "bound" to happen, just as the spells of fairy-women were "binding" (302).

Penelope, or "She Whose Face is Veiled," a title of the weaving Fate-goddess, is cast in the *Odyssey* as Odysseus' wife who weaves and unweaves the tapestry of his life, never cutting it off, thus saving his life while deceiving the vulturous suitors (Walker, 782). Arachne, the "Spider" or "Spinner," was a totem of Athena the Fate-weaver: "Classical writers misinterpreted old images of Athene with her spider-totem and web, and constructed the legend of Arachne, a mortal maid whose skill in weaving outshone even that of the Goddess. Therefore Athene turned her into a spider" (Walker, 54). Obviously, Walker's encyclopedia itself is a re-forming of stories turned sideways or upside down in the patriarchal literature; such re-forming companions me in my own efforts, provides alternate wefts for weaving across the warps of human experience.

Spider Woman is another of the great weaving goddesses of the earth and its creatures; she is co-creator, according to the Hopi, with Taiowa, the Sun God, and she is their all-wise, all-powerful guardian. She taught the Navajo women how to weave. In her book, *The Mother's Songs: Images of God the Mother*, the artist Meinrad Craighead writes alongside her painting called "Web": "In the beginning, as one of the old stories says, there was nothing but Spiderwoman. She spun two threads and where they crossed she sat singing and her singing made everything and held it all together" (31).

Craighead goes on to speak of this image in connection with a cherished happy memory of sitting alone with her mother during one childhood afternoon. Her mother was silently sewing and she was drawing: "I ask, 'What do you think about when you sew?' 'I don't think. I am remembering,' she replies. 'When I am sewing, I hold you all together'" (31).

Each one of us probably has a network of these spinning-weaving mothers and sisters from our own trove of myths and stories as well as from our own personal experiences—our own Spider Woman-mothers as well as our own Mary and Martha sister-selves, among others. I invite you to make your own weaver-web (a special kind of family tree—why not draw or paint it?), and then to reflect upon it.

"Women's work" has often been omitted from the records and we are all the poorer for that. Still, as we re-weave our own lives, our own networks, we enrich human possibility. As Schüssler Fiorenza writes in the concluding pages of *In Memory of Her*: "This history of women as the people of God must be exposed as a history of oppression as well as a history of conversion and liberation. When I speak of the *ekklesia* of women, I have in mind women of the past and of the present, women who have acted and still act in the power of the life-giving Sophia-Spirit" (350).

Including these women and their work in a history become not just *her*story, but *our*story, we re-weave our household until it becomes more and more a reflection of the Household Jesus teaches us about in the Martha and Mary stories.

Journaling Out Some Knots

In drawing out the network of my own spinner-weaver mothers and sisters, one of the painful things I learned was that during some periods of my life, I felt widely separated from them. At one point, in my pondering of this network and some periods of disconnection from it, I reached a crisis and wrote about it in my journal:

> Today I learned a valuable lesson. It began yesterday when I was writing about women's work, about my own network, and my loneliness through so much of my search for meaning, for wholeness. This morning I came back to the library and wrote more about my anger; yesterday's work seems to have opened old wounds—I had to realize just how *hard* that time I'd been focusing upon had been. So this morning I found myself getting more and more angry and sad, looking back over what was a career-damaging anti-nepotism situation I'd been cast into as a married woman with a partner in the same field. The situation had led to a depressing confusion about every aspect of my personhood.
>
> Clearly, when we begin to "re-weave" our lives, it is inevitable, especially for women, that we are bound

to find thwarting sexisms and circumstances; they present to us the very real temptation to re-write, saying "it was bitterness and thwarting and very little else," at least for some periods. That is what I faced myself this a.m. in the deepest of my depression as I counted up the ways I'd been cheated of what I felt I'd earned or been eligible for because I was a daughter not a son, a married and not a single woman, and a female person in the culture generally. It would have been quite easy to slide right over into abject self-deprecation and loathing—a real wallow in the "pity pit."

It is important to ask how we are vulnerable when we view the worst of what has happened to us and to our mothers and sisters in our attempts to become authentic, integrated selves. What are the dangers that lurk in our bad memory recalling? And how may we protect ourselves from getting stuck in such draining negativity? I think of Jesus' parable about the man who was exorcised of a devil only to have his clean, empty house taken over by seven more. How can we keep our house, once cleansed, from being taken over by devilishness instead of the positiveness we intend?

I tried to pray in response to the state I found myself in. I wasn't very good about it, but I thought of something else to divert my downward slide, and that was to throw the coins for the *I Ching*. I have found that this simple practice often helps me to think freshly and affirmatively about my situation. One of the reasons may be that when I get around to doing this, I am already prepared to get out of my rut and get on with whatever I'm doing. But this was one of the most remarkable answers I ever received when consulting it. I posed this question: "How can I do this work of mine with more joy?"

My hexagram was "Ken," or "Keeping Still." I read the interpretation in Sam Reifler's *I Ching: A New Interpretation for Modern Times* and it was perfect (except for gender reference, which I changed):

> One mountain above another.
> The superior woman does not let her mind
> stray from her immediate activities.
> Her back is at rest
> and she is free from self-consciousness.
> She walks about her courtyard
> without noticing the people in it.
>
> NO MISTAKES (229).

The interpretation explains that if the spine is totally relaxed it shows that the mind has overcome the greatest psychological stress, the illusion of ego, "that fosters woman's characteristic alienation from the world around her." And wow, was I feeling alienated!

> Your direction is essentially spiritual. Whatever problems you have are only shadows of your spiritual struggle. If you perceive a problem, then your problem is that you perceive it as a problem in the first place; you know better. You understand and have experienced the stillness of this hexagram. The "question" about which you have consulted the I Ching oracle is predicated on concepts and values which YOU KNOW have no substance in a state of keeping still. And, keeping still, at rest, at one with time and space, is your Tao. . . . You are on the path. . . . Do Hatha-Yoga, or the Japanese physical discipline *hara*, or another system that regards the body as an animal form of divine principles, rather than a beast of burden for Time (229–30).

I had the grace available after reading this to know I had to re-weave my pattern—I, as all other humans, have had nasty periods of life. I have much to forgive in others and in myself; what I need to do is to face the wrong, forgive, and then go on. We can be tempted by regression when we trace present situations to their roots, but if we are wise and graced, we know that we know better, that if we can only be content to be still, we will know that God is with us, that our Now is an abundant fulfillment of our lives. And so we can go on weaving, with lighter shoulders, with unencumbered minds. We need to name these things that have been knots and breakages for us, but we need even more to know that God's love untangles and mends them; then we may go on about our journey-weaving. (In some faith communities, such reconciliation is effected by the practice of "healing of memories.")

Having had this experience and pondered it in my journal, I understood some of the perils of re-visiting times of darkness; however, the journey seemed necessary and not impossible to turn toward Light. I am sure the Weaver Angels, the Seraphic Spinsters, had something to do with this!

Chapter 5

Re-Patterning the Martha-Mary Web: Re-Weaving with Theological Imagination

> *Such imagination is the power of the Holy Spirit to bring to new life whatever has become fossilized* (Elisabeth Moltmann-Wendel, 10).

Following the pattern I have established in this weaving, I have addressed the stereotypes which Martha and Mary in their stories have called up for myself and others as individuals first; I have tried to ask, "What must I search and understand in myself before I can speak to and with others about this issue?" So in the previous chapter I attended to the stereotype-knots I apprehended as most disturbing in the weaving. Now I turn to others for their commentaries on my sisters Martha and Mary as a way to extend and deepen our exploration, as a way to incorporate further community. I wondered, assuming my scholarly role, how others had woven the Martha-Mary-Jesus network with art, history, and theology, for example. What body of knowledge had already been amassed for us by other seekers?

Some Theological Re-Imaginings

A. Moltmann-Wendel Re-Imagines

Elisabeth Moltmann-Wendel provided me with many answers to my questions in her study, *The Women Around Jesus*.

In this work she discusses the "forgotten art" of theological imagination. She writes that it is "necessary in a church and a theology which has lost touch with women, if new life is to be given to the gospel of liberation. With this kind of imagination, theology which has become abstract and has lost touch with women can again become what it once was, and affect the whole person. Such imagination is the power of the Holy Spirit to bring to new life whatever has become fossilized" (9–10). She proceeds to demonstrate what I found to be the truly heartening power of applied theological imagination. Her first two chapters are about, first, Martha, and second, Mary of Bethany. She follows a pattern of looking first through the Bible, then in art and in church history to find a variety of illustrations that "show us the 'other' woman who is hidden from us by the patriarchal view of history and the blinkers worn by the church, and should guide us back to the other possibilities offered by the Christian traditions" (11). Moltmann-Wendel reminds us that from Luther to the present-day commentators, Mary has been "the type of the contemplative," the person "who is good and righteous before God because she listened to the word" (20). Martha, however, "has been made the patron saint of housewives and cooks, and been given a saint's day (29 July). Even now there are Martha Organizations, for domestics in manses and guest-houses. A women's movement in England which opposes the emancipation of women is actually called the Martha Movement" (20).

It is this latter kind of Martha which the Canadian writer Margaret Atwood portrays in her best-selling 1986 novel, *The Handmaid's Tale*. She imagines a future society of rude and inflexibly divided class/gender roles for women and men; all the Marthas wear dull green garb and are domestic drones, a grim reduction of Martha as the prototypical busy housewife. Here we see the horror of a society which deprives women (and men) of all their imaginative resources, carrying all our patriarchal stereotypes into a deadly reduction to absurdity.

Although the nineteenth century reclaimed Martha as an image of active Christianity, especially for social workers and deaconesses, Moltmann-Wendel notes that Martha and her housekeeping skills ''are still on the periphery of our Christianity'' as the ''Martha Houses are on the periphery of the great deaconess organizations'' (22).

Yet if we look at the Johannine stories about the sisters and not just the Lukan version which our Christian tradition has followed, much to Martha's detriment, we find a forgotten Martha. Focusing on Martha's confession of Jesus as the Christ when he comes to raise Lazarus from the dead (John 11:27), as other feminist theologians (for example, Haughton and Schüssler Fiorenza) have, Moltmann-Wendel celebrates John's re-imaging of Martha: ''He restores to life the aggressive, disturbing, sage, active Martha who went against all the conventions: mistress of the house, housewife, apostle, the woman who stands beside Peter in her own right,'' she who was ''the first to hear that Jesus is the resurrection and the life'' (26, 28).

B. Eckhart Re-Imagines

In the fourteenth and fifteenth centuries, Martha was praised in literature and especially in art as a competent, spiritual, and thoroughly admirable person. About 1300, a Dominican preacher and mystic, Meister Eckhart of Hochheim, preached a sermon on Martha and Mary which he titled, ''When Our Work Becomes a Spiritual Work Working in the World.'' In this sermon, he turns our contemporary images of negative Martha and positive Mary completely upside down. Eckhart describes Martha as one who ''possessed a mature, well-established virtue . . . our dear Martha, and with her, all God's friends are '*among* cares' but not '*within* cares.' In this connection, activity in time is just as noble as any kind of linking of self and God. For it carries us just as close as possible to the highest thing, except for the vision of God in his pure nature'' (483).

Besides, writes Eckhart (I imagine his eyes twinkling in iconoclastic glee), ''We cherish the suspicion that our dear Mary somehow had sat there more out of a feeling of pleasure than for spiritual gain. Therefore Martha said: 'Lord, tell her to get up!' For she feared that Mary would remain in this feeling of pleasure and make no further progress'' (480). He finds Jesus' statement to Martha not a reproof but rather a consolation that Mary ''would become the way she wished her to be'' (480). Martha ''possessed a mature, well-established virtue and an undisturbed disposition that was unhindered by all things. For this reason she wanted her sister to be placed in the same situation. . . . Out of a mature depth of soul she wanted Mary to be in everything that has to do with eternal happiness. On this account Christ says: '*One thing* is necessary!' What is this *one thing*? It is the One, and that is God'' (483).

Matthew Fox, in his commentary in *Breakthrough: Meister Eckhart's Creation Spirituality in New Translation*, expounds upon Eckhart's development of a theology of work as a spirituality:

> Contrary to many traditional exegeses of the Martha/Mary story and the theology of action/contemplation that was behind these interpretations, Eckhart believes that contemplation is not better than, nor, in the mature person, even different from work. For work too carries us just as close as possible to the highest thing, except for the vision of God in his pure nature. Compassion and the works born of compassion are themselves acts of contemplation. This is the fullness of spiritual maturity: to be in the world, active in the world, and yet not hindered by these actions from being always in God (489).

Re-Imaging in Paintings and Legends

For various social, political, and religious reasons, Martha's orientation toward action drew many followers to her. Women's religious orders, the Humiliati, the Franciscans, and smaller brotherhoods made her the patron saint of churches and communities, and artists frequently portrayed her (Moltmann-Wendel 33). In a side chapel in the Church of Santa Croce in Florence, Giovanni di Milano depicts her as the host at Bethany, illuminated by an inner light; in St. Martha's Church in Lugano (fourteenth century), ''She has the spiritual status of a guardian Madonna'' (Moltmann-Wendel, 35). ''The Martha of this period,'' writes Moltmann-Wendel, ''often has a vessel in her hand. This is the famous jar of oil, which did not really go with her but with her sister, who was thought to have anointed Jesus. However, the jar of oil has become a vessel, a symbol, of the woman. Her body is a vessel. Her implements are vessels. Martha, the *magna mater*, becomes the embodiment of the mature, powerful, creative woman who fulfills herself and makes her own contribution'' (35–37).

One unusual painting by the Dominican Fra Angelico shows Mary and Martha at Gethsemane. Peter, James, and John are asleep, but the women keep watch. Mary bows her head reading a book, but Martha is ''fully alert, casting questioning looks at Mary and praying with uplifted hands, adopting the same attitude as the sorely tired Jesus in the background'' (Moltmann-Wendel, 38).

Some of the portraits of the two sisters depict the legend which tells of how they, their brother Lazarus, and St. Maximinus were expelled from Palestine, put on a leaky raft, and in this way reached France where they all did missionary work. In *The Golden Legend of Jacobus De Voragine*, we learn that Lazarus became bishop of Marseilles; Martha gained permission to remain in the place where she vanquished the dragon of Tarascon. There, along the Rhone River, a great community of religious women grew up around her, and a basilica was built in honour of the Blessed Virgin Mary (392). Even now, one may visit the Church of St. Martha in Tarascon and pray in the chapel where Martha's reliquary sits upon the altar or in the crypt below where her remains are said to be sealed in the great sarcophagus. When I worshipped there with my family in June of 1989, I lit a candle upon Martha's reliquary altar. As we left the church a wedding party was entering—a sweet, exuberant sign of Martha's spirit in the world, I felt.

The theme I find most fascinating in these late medieval and early Renaissance depictions is that of Martha defeating the dragon. As a sign of this wondrous theme, I weave Martha's sash, or girdle, as it is referred to, across the loom. In the por-

PAROISSE SAINTE·MARTHE
13150 TARASCON

trayals of her conquering the dragon, she usually holds a pitcher and a holy water sprinkler (aspergillum) or cross in one hand, and her girdle, symbol of purity, with which she binds the dragon, in the other. Moltmann-Wendel suggests that in contrast with male dragonslayers "Martha marks the symbolic beginning of another way of dealing with evil: not its annihilation but its redemption, 'the transformation of the underside,' as Erich Neumann puts it" (46).

Considering Martha in this new light, as a gentle dragon conqueror, I was moved to write this poem:

MARTHA'S WAY

George's way with dragons—
    all that metal-shelled
    lance-armed strategy
    for goring—
was the only way I knew
until I met Martha.

"The dragon is a lord of water"
said she. "I sprinkle him with
holy water to melt his anger."

"The dragon is a lord of fire,"
said she. "I encircle him with my sash,
and lead him home to my hearth."

"The dragon is a lord of earth"
said she. "Why spindle him dead
to one fixed point, when alive
he'll be with me wherever I go?"

"The dragon is a lord of air"
said she. "In wind, in clouds, and
in rain, I see him stretching
from earth to heaven."

This emancipating image of Martha disappeared with the Reformation and Counter Reformation and was replaced entirely by the image of George. But Moltmann-Wendel's exercise of theological imagination in restoring this lost Martha to me and to others gives me courage; both she and this Martha she uncovers are members of my network of weaver women. Mary, too, belongs in my network, but I want to "name" her more fully when I write about discipleship in chapter 6.

Here is another thread of commentary that delights me and teaches me a fresh way to view Mary and Martha. It is a desert wisdom story collected by Yoshi Nomura about a brother who comes to visit Abba Silvanus at Mount Sinai. When he sees the brothers at work, he says to the old man: "Do not work for the food that perishes. For Mary has chosen the good part." The old man calls a disciple to give this brother a book and an empty cell. At the end of the day the visitor is very hungry and wonders why no one has called him to eat. Abba Silvanus explains that he himself and the others are not so spiritual as to be able to go without earthly food and so must work for it, but since he, the visitor, has chosen the good part, they didn't think he wanted to eat earthly food. "When the brother heard this, he repented and said: Mary certainly needed Martha, and it is really by Martha's help that Mary is praised" (Nomura, 42–43).

Commentary from *The Cloud of Unknowing*

The unknown author of the fourteenth century *The Cloud of Unknowing* adds a gentle "middle way" for understanding Martha and Mary. Whereas the author rejoices that Mary sits at Jesus' feet "in perfect stillness with her heart's secret, joyous love intent upon that *cloud of unknowing* between her and her God," the author ascertains that "Martha's chores were holy and important," and that her complaints came from not realizing then what Mary was doing (71, 73).

Furthermore, the author asserts that there are only two ways of life in the Church, the active and the contemplative, and these two combine into a third way:

> Taken as a whole, there are three parts, three ascending stages. . . . The first stage is the good and upright Christian life in which love is predominantly active in the corporal works of mercy. In the second, a person begins to meditate on spiritual truths regarding his own sinfulness, the Passion of Christ and the joys of eternity. The first way is good but the second is better, for here the active and contemplative life begin to converge. They merge in a sort of spiritual kinship, becoming sisters like Martha and Mary (76).

For the active person, the second stage "is as far as . . . [he or she] may advance in contemplation except for the occasional intervention of special grace"; for the contemplative person, this "middle ground" may be revisited, but only "on rare occasions and at the demand of great need" (*The Cloud*, 76). "In the third stage a person enters the dark *cloud of unknowing* where in secret and alone he centers all his love on God. . . . This is the best part belonging to Mary. It is surely obvious now why our Lord did not say to Martha, 'Mary has chosen the best life.' There are only two ways of life and, as I said, when a choice is only between two one may not be called best. But our Lord says, 'Mary has chosen the best *part* and it shall not be taken from her' '' (76).

For *The Cloud of Unknowing* author, the first and second parts are ''good and holy but they will cease with the passing of this mortal life''; the third part, however, ''though it begins on earth, it is eternal'' (76–77). Our Lord's reply to Martha is the reply to active persons who complain about contemplative persons (including the author, who refers to the latter as ''us''): ''Let him speak for us as he did for Mary when he said, 'Martha, Martha.' He is saying, 'Listen, all you who live the active life. Be diligent in the works of the first and second parts, working now in one, now in another. Or if you are so inclined, courageously undertake both together. But do not interfere with my contemplative friends, for you do not understand what afflicts them. Leave them in peace. Do not begrudge them the leisure of the third and best part which is Mary's'' (77).

We Re-Imagine the Sisters' Portraits

And so we weave a way together. Reflect upon these stories, these images, and journal or draw with them. Which of the commentaries do you prefer? Which ones touch your life particularly? Or do you need to write your own? What conclusions are you drawing (literally or otherwise) about ''women's work'' as you weave along with this chapter?

One of the exercises I set for myself was to think about Martha's and Mary's hands. Martha is often shown carrying keys, a ladle, a jar, and sometimes, as I have mentioned in relation to her dragon-slaying, a pitcher, a cross or holy water sprinkler and her girdle, or sash, a sign of purity. I thought of Mary's hands as empty, in a gesture of prayerfulness, or perhaps with a holy text in them. In one drawing, I saw Mary's hands as open and receiving, Martha's as full and giving; I drew them in a circle which I divided into the yin-yang interlocking ''teardrop'' shapes, and thus it seemed that they were related in a dynamic reciprocity, a continuity of giving-receiving. In a later drawing, this giving-receiving image changed into a pitcher (Martha) pouring into a bowl (Mary), a representation I found even more satisfying than the previous one. I tried using color in the drawing, too, and found red fitted my sense of Martha's active nature, and blue fitted Mary; when these two colors meet and blend together they make purple, a color symbolic of higher spirituality, of meditation and holiness.

Schüssler Fiorenza Re-Imagines and I Respond

As I follow the pattern of network-naming and collecting of various interpretations of the story of Mary and Martha in this weaving, I mention one more. Elisabeth Schüssler Fiorenza's feminist critique of the Lukan Martha-Mary story sharply criticizes what she finds as the patriarchal bias of the text and its interpretations. While her critique may help us to avoid oppression-continuing readings of this text, what I find most useful is her articulation of a ''hermeneutics of creative actualization and celebration.'' Used with intelligent and sensitive awareness, such a hermeneutic ''allows women to enter the biblical text with the help of historical imagination, narrative amplifications, artistic recreations and liturgical celebrations (''A Feminist Critical Interpretation for Liberation,'' 33–34).

It is my intent that this weaving-writing-imagining a way together is an exercise of this ''hermeneutics of creative actuali-

zation and celebration'' as well as of what Elisabeth Moltmann-Wendel calls ''theological imagination.'' I *do* find positive value in the Lukan text, but as my dialogues testify, this value often comes as a result of the struggle I am pushed to engage in to re-construct, to re-weave my life away from the imprisoning conventional interpretations given this text.

I would summarize my position this way: I know that being a female member of a patriarchal culture has warped my sense of personhood, has led me to internalize patterns of self- and other-denigration which I must unweave in order to achieve any kind of health or wholeness. I know that in my culture I share this ''inferiorization,'' if you will, with all other persons who are not favored by being white, male, heterosexual, Anglo-Saxon Protestants, of economic independence and of sound mind and body as well. But, I also believe, as a Christian, that the Spirit leads me to re-warp my life-loom so that the threads being re-woven reveal a pattern I may truly celebrate. This text-textile unity I am weaving here is testimony, I believe, that this writing from Luke leads me to an ultimately positive struggle; it is problematic but not in an annihilating way. If I have unconsciously swallowed the ''raw deal'' it represents in conventional terms, now I am consciously ridding myself, and hopefully others, of its toxins.

In spite of what Elisabeth Schüssler Fiorenza calls the ''androcentric dualism and patriarchal prejudice inherent in

the original story,'' I find in it a positive challenge (33). We must meet head-on the past and present historical reality that makes the world-weaving ''women's work'' of the household difficult to perform as empowered persons. The stories of Martha and Mary challenge us all to re-consider what our own ''woman's work'' is and how we may engage in it in a way that allows the radiance of God to shine through. I find the Lukan story a testament to Jesus' insistence upon being with us in this often demeaning area of our lives; he accepts our invitation to be his guest and then he shows us how to transform this work so that we may be *his* guests. He proclaims within this household (as in all households) a message which reverses the patriarchal society's ideas of power. He accomplishes this by a complete re-visioning of the role of service in his Household.

As we consider the model of servant in Christian discipleship, we see an historic progression from freedom to slavery in regard to ''women's work.'' Elizabeth Tetlow writes: ''As long as servant remained the primary model for Christian ministry women were able to minister on the same basis as men. When at the close of the New Testament period the Christian model of servant was replaced by Jewish models of presbyter and bishop, and in the 2nd century the Old Testament model of levitical priesthood was applied to ecclesiastical office, women came to be excluded from the official ministry of the church'' (78–79).

Now we have the task of reclaiming Jesus' model of servanthood.

Chapter 6

The Pattern of Discipleship:
Threads of Mature Commitment

Mary took a pound of costly ointment of pure nard and anointed the feet of Jesus and wiped his feet with her hair; and the house was filled with the fragrance of the ointment (John 12:3).

In the two previous chapters I have considered issues that seem to me to precede fully mature discipleship; stereotyping involves traps and tangles that must be clearly identified, re-imagined, and then rewoven. Once we are able to claim ourselves from these tangles however, we must take what knowledge, what renewed joy we have found into the domain of discipleship, it is here that our Martha-Mary selves may at last weave with all their being for God's glory.

In the Household as Jesus re-visioned it, the powerful were those who were able to wholly give themselves into loving service. Within this radical framework and precisely at this point in my writing, I felt it necessary to re-consider the meanings of service, of servanthood, and of discipleship. Though in my investigation of the biblical roots I emphasize the scholarship focusing upon women as disciples, my intent is to address this topic for all of us, for the Mary and Martha selves within us whether we are women or men.

In Luke, Martha speaks to Jesus: " 'Lord, do you not care that my sister has left me to serve alone? Tell her then to help me.' But the Lord answered her, 'Martha, Martha, you are anxious and troubled about many things; one thing is needful.' "

There are three words that leap out at me from this passage as I ponder it: "serve," "alone," and "anxious" (or "troubled"). These three words bring up terribly demanding questions: What is right for us to be doing? With whom, if anyone, do we need to be companioned in our doing? How may we deal with the inevitable anxiety our doing brings to us?

About these three words my Martha self voices some of her worries: "How do I know if I've done enough?" "What if I'm left to do all the tedious, invisible tasks (while others do the "glory-grabbing"), and I get angry when no one thanks me (and I get upset with my own pettiness!)?" "What if I charge in and work so hard I suffer 'burn-out'?" "What if I lose my focus and get confused about what Jesus really wants me to do?" "What if I can't inspire others around me to get up and act as directly as I think is right?"

My Mary self has her own set of worries: "What if I feel alone in what I do?" "What if I lose ways to connect with Martha's action?" "What if my own quiet, prayerful discipline begins to feel ineffective to me?" "What if I cannot show others the necessity of balancing action with contemplation?"

Investigating the Meaning of *Diakonia,* "Service"

To begin, I weave onto the loom the beginning threads of a pattern of service revealed in our texts. Our English word "serve" is translated here from the Greek *diakonein,* which elsewhere, in the form *diēkonoun,* is translated as "provided for" (see the passage following Luke 8:1 in which Jesus is accompanied by "the twelve, certain women . . . and many others, who provided for them out of their means"). Elsewhere *diēkonoun* is translated as "ministered to" (see Mark 15:40-42, describing the women at the crucifixion, mentioning by name Mary Magdalene, Mary, mother of James the younger and Joses, and Salome "who, when he was in Galilee, followed him, and ministered to him"). We note then that the meaning of *diakonia* and its other forms in the New Testament "denotes service and is synonymous with ministry" (Tetlow, 68).

We see in these Greek words the basis of our English words "deacon" and "diaconate"; in Acts 6:1-6, we have the account of the first commissioning of deacons "to serve tables" ("to serve" as *diakonein*) in assistance to the disciples. The tasks of the deacons in early Christianity were much the same as those the women, including Martha, undertook (Swidler, 180).

As Elizabeth Tetlow notes, "In hellenistic Greek the basic meaning of the word *diakonia* is service. This service often took the form of service at table. In Greek culture no form of service was desirable or meaningful. In the Old Testament and semitic culture, on the other hand, service was honorable in proportion to the greatness of the master served" (68).

Lest we take the passage cited above, Acts 6:1-6, as a statement of hierarchy of disciples over deacons, we note that Jesus emphasizes that he is among us "as one who serves." Consider these words from Luke about one of the events at the Last Supper:

> A dispute also arose among them, which of them was to be regarded as the greatest. And he said to them, "The kings of the Gentiles exercise lordship over them; and those in authority over them are called benefactors. But not so with you; rather let the greatest among you become as the youngest, and the leader as one who *serves* [*diakonōn*]. For which is the greater, one who sits at table, or one who *serves* [*diakonōn*]? Is it not the one who sits at table? But I am among you as one who *serves* [again, *diakonōn*]" (Luke 22:24-27).

Again, I cite Tetlow's words in summation: "All *diakonia* ultimately derives from Jesus' own ministry as servant" (68). See also Philippians 2:5-7: "Have this mind among yourselves, which you have in Christ Jesus, who, though he was in the form of God, did not count equality with God a thing to be grasped, but emptied himself, taking the form of a servant [here *doulos*, "slave"!], being born in the likeness of men."

Recall Martha's complaint: "My sister has left me to serve alone." We have only to think of similar complaints we have made. Where are our helpers when we most need them? Why, if we are conscientious workers, do we so often find ourselves doing the work alone and resenting it? ("If only I could get some help around here!") What is to save us from becoming filled with bitterness and self-pity?

Jesus gives us an important message when he says (Luke 22:27), "But I am among you as one who serves." He *was* helping Martha if she had but noticed? Ask, seek, knock—"Martha, all you had to do was to ask *me* and you would have received all the help you needed to keep from being anxious and distracted"—is that what Jesus might have said? Or Jesus might have gently reminded her that they were sharing hospitality. Jesus might have said: "Martha, you are my sister in service. Be at peace with your work, do it always *with me.*" If she would somehow calm down and do things simply, slowly, and patiently, she would be a receiver as well as a giver (see how she becomes a mirror for us in those times when we are so relentlessly bent upon giving that we become a parody of our original intent!).

Elisabeth Moltmann-Wendel connects "serving" Jesus with adopting his style of life. In reference to the healing of Peter's mother-in-law (Mark 1:29-31), Moltmann-Wendel notes that this woman's response to Jesus' healing is service, entering into his way of life in concrete action (68). If Martha will only understand that Jesus is offering her this transformative possibility of service in his name!

One of the commentators on this text says, in essence, "Martha, don't be distracted, Mary has the main course all ready; just bring a few olives, or even one and it will be sufficient." As one of my friends put it, Jesus might well have said, "Martha, come on in and sit with us; we'll just send out for pizza."

Now I am thinking of all the ways in which I am responsible to serve—I think of my "real" job of teaching, and of obvious Christian service as an elder in my church; I think of all the informal ways I serve in relationships as wife, mother, friend, teacher, sister, and daughter; I think of service in various organizations; I think of my writing, of my prayers, of my very thoughts. I even think of gardening and of caring for our cat, Leo. In curiosity, I set myself the task of making a kind of pie-diagram of my life in terms of the forms of service I performed, on a daily, weekly, monthly, and yearly basis. (Have you ever tried to do this? Can you imagine it?)

As I struggled with this task (and I found myself making not one but several diagrams, one for each time category, two for each day so that I could work in the two twelve-hour cycles) I became rather overwhelmed. I noticed that I hadn't even put recreation on the wheel—as though recreation had nothing to do with service! One question I had was whether I should or could call all this activity "service" or even "discipleship." Even thinking about that question revealed to me just how separate I was holding these categories from most of my life's doings. It was easy enough to call my explicitly church-connected work "service" or "discipleship," but much less easy to so categorize my tending plants, washing clothes, making meals, preparing classes, or writing letters. I asked myself why this was so. At first, I had no satisfactory answer. Part of the process of this entire Martha-Mary work was still unwinding for me, slowly enough that I could see no pattern.

I was asking this question of why I had assumed a separation of works and "service" as I began a new semester and as I was embarking on many new projects. I was feeling less anxious than in some former semesters' beginnings, but I clearly had moments of real anxiety—how would I get that new lecture in the shape I wanted it to be, in time? How would we find a theme that really worked for our women's retreat? How would I ever keep to the ambitious schedule I had set myself for writing or stick to the (nearly impossible) physical and spiritual self-improvement programs I had designed? How would I get all this housework done?

On top of all that, I allowed myself to be distracted by all sorts of self-pitying thoughts about empty-nesting, about the increasing frustrations of being a middle-aged person, about my students' apparent lack of seriousness, about the state of the world with all the stupidity, terror, and pollution the media daily reported to me. It became clear to me that I was allowing distractions to rise up and rule me.

I was being Martha at her worst, sure enough. Clearly, I was complaining, "Lord, do you not care that everyone has left me to serve alone? Tell them all to help me (and to recognize what a terrifically hard-working server I am as well!)." Now what was it that Jesus wanted me to do to get back in touch with "the one thing needful"?

Let me simply say that at this point in the writing, I found myself with little inspiration for the weaving. I felt I was waiting for a new shipment of yarn, and I was impatient because, in my estimation, it was taking far too long to arrive. Every time I tried to concentrate on the weaving, I felt how greatly I had empowered my distractions. I wanted to attend to this work, but other things kept me occupied (I allowed and even chose these "other things," not always able to say that they were less important than this work). Sometimes I understood the "work" as being only this particular manuscript and felt dismal; other (preferred) times I understood the "work" in its larger dimensions and felt hopeful.

In an event of wonderful grace, during a Bible study of the Gospel of John at our church, it dawned upon me that my distractions were an excuse and a stalling from my personal encounter with the newness that Jesus as Christ offered to me. In John 3:3 I read: "Truly, truly, I say to you, unless one is born anew, [s]he cannot see the kingdom of God."

We know that the fears of falling and glaring lights and blaring noises give an infant anxiety. For the most part, though, given the gift of loving parents, a newborn lives in a world of dreamy warmth and ready food, a state of being-taken-care-of that is astoundingly luxurious. When I think about my proclivity to let anxiety scatter and distract me, I imagine an infant who refuses to be fed or held or loved when all is freely and abundantly offered. How ungrateful, stubborn, and foolish was I going to persist in being?

"Martha, Martha, you are anxious and troubled about many

things; one thing is needful." Jesus gently calls to Martha, hoping to turn her from her distractions back to God's loving presence, which he brings into her house. Does that mean he wishes her to stop serving and sit at his feet with Mary? Perhaps, but I think not. Her service is necessary, yet there is something she deeply misses in her effort to serve her master and friend, and the lack of that something makes her serving incomplete and even counter-productive.

Jesus calls Martha's name twice. In so doing, he calls her into relationship with him and reminds her of her discipleship (see the parable of the Good Shepherd in John 10:1-5; Jesus compares his disciples to sheep who know their shepherd's voice when he calls them by name). In her book, *Women and Spirituality*, Carol Ochs writes a passage I find helpfully relevant to the separate claims Jesus is asking Martha to join: "Somehow, within our own being, we must balance the two claims on us of responsibility and relationship. To choose one, as traditional spirituality has done, at the expense of the other is to formulate a spirituality that is inadequate to the needs of a full humanity" (109). I believe that Jesus is calling Martha to be fully present to him and also to her sister Mary, to the present situation in all its human/divine dimensions. As David Swindall aptly summarized in a sermon on Mary and Martha, Martha needs to learn how to *choose* to do whatever she needs to do, and to let go of distraction in order to do it to God's glory.

Jesus seeks to teach Martha his compassionate art of being "distracted from distraction by distraction." I borrow this phrase from Tony Stoneburner, who writes, "Considering the gospels as their authors have constructed them, I see Jesus as distracted from distraction by distraction, as responsive to persons in their need and faithful to God in each new event" (91).

Paul Tillich, in a sermon called "Our Ultimate Concern," addresses the words Jesus speaks to Martha as ones we need to hear. "Martha's way is not contemptible," he writes. "On the contrary, it is the way which keeps the world running. . . . But they [her concerns] do not demand *infinite* attention, *un-*

conditional devotion, *ultimate* passion" (152–53). In conclusion, Tillich writes:

> *But Mary was infinitely concerned.* This is the one thing needed.
> If, in the power and passion of such an ultimate concern, we look at our finite concerns, at the Martha sphere of life, everything seems the same and yet everything is changed. We are still concerned about all these things, but differently—the anxiety is gone! But its power is broken; it cannot destroy us any more. He who is grasped by the one thing that is needed has the many things under his feet. They concern him but not ultimately, and when he loses them he does not lose the one thing he needs and that cannot be taken from him (159–160).

"Everything seems the same and yet everything is changed." In those words Tillich describes for me the revisioning of the world that Jesus' teaching gives to us when we commit ourselves to being his disciples, his servants.

Jesus' model of service is quintessentially compassionate, we might say. He asks us to be at once simply and completely human *and* simply and completely divine. If we, in service, embrace compassionately all the needs, joys, and sufferings that are our human lot, doing this in his Spirit, then we center ourselves in "the one thing necessary."

Women as Disciples in Luke–Acts

Seeking to deepen my understanding of discipleship in terms of Martha and Mary and the "women's work" they share with me and others, I turn again to the scripture passages: first, the domestic story I have been focusing on which is found only in the third gospel, Luke 10:38-42. (In the ensuing discussion, which leads from this Lukan story to the Johannine ones, I rely predominantly on the two interpretations I have found most useful: Elizabeth Meier Tetlow's *Women and Ministry in the New Testament: Called to Serve*, and Raymond E. Brown's "Roles of Women in the Fourth Gospel.")

The entire tenth chaper of Luke emphasizes the theme of discipleship. It begins with the commissioning of the seventy (or seventy-two; there are authorities for both numbers) who are sent out two by two to preach and to heal. Their instructions are basically the same ones given to the Twelve in Matthew 10:5-15 and Mark 6:7-11 where they are also sent out in pairs. The New Testament usage of the word for *disciple* (*mathetes* in reference to the Twelve and others; only once specifically referring to a woman, in reference to Tabitha ["which means Dorcas or Gazelle"] of Joppa, Acts 9:36) generally means "learner or apprentice," or a "follower, adherent" ("Disciple," *Encyclopedia Dictionary of the Bible*).

"It is not denied that Mary and Martha are disciples," writes Tetlow (104). I notice that Martha and Mary are indeed a pair and wonder if they do not epitomize between them the ideal qualities of a disciple, their story coming as it does at the end of a gospel chapter devoted to discipleship. Yet not only Tetlow, but Schüssler Fiorenza, Brown, and others note that the picture of Martha's and Mary's discipleship is skewed by Luke's attitude toward women's "proper" sphere of service in the church. "In Acts as in the third gospel Luke focused on the passive role of women" (Tetlow, 107). Although "Luke did go beyond contemporary rabbinic Judaism in permitting a woman [Mary] to learn Torah," he "did not permit either of the women [Mary or Martha] a role of proclamation" (Tetlow, 104).

In her discussion of biblical foundations of ministry, Tetlow speaks of two major traditions of ministry in the Old Testament, both alive in late Judaism. These were priesthood, which was completely closed to women by law, and ministry of word, which was at least theoretically open to women (Tetlow, 44). Jesus' ministry of word through suffering service provided a new and freeing model:

> The ministry of servant was new and unique and had not been connected with any formal religious office in the history of Judaism. . . . As long as servant remained the primary model for Christian ministry women were able to minister on the same basis as men. When, at the close of the New Testament period the Christian model of servant was replaced by Jewish models

of presbyter and bishop, and in the second century the Old Testament model of levitical priesthood was applied to ecclesiastical office, women came to be excluded from the official ministry of the Church (Tetlow, 78–79).

In other words,

> Luke–Acts seems to reflect a situation in the Church similar to that found in the pastoral epistles near the end of the first century. Women had long been free to exercise a major and influential role in the ministry of the Church. But by this time the men were becoming weary of this situation and were seeking to keep women quiet within the community and to restrict their role to a passive one, although they were still eager to benefit materially from the resources of well-to-do women (Tetlow, 109).

Martha and Mary as Disciples in *John*

A. Martha's Pattern Flowers

Let us compare the stories of Martha and Mary in John to the one in Luke. In discussing approaches to "the biblical evidence pertinent to the contemporary debate about the role of women in the Church," Raymond E. Brown states that he has chosen to focus upon John; he does so "because of the perceptive corrective that the Evangelist offers to some ecclesiastical attitudes of his time—his should be a voice heard and reflected upon when we are discussing new roles for women in the Church today" (688–89).

Although the Gospel of John, like the Synoptics, was written during the second half of the first century, it draws upon other and "comparably reliable and primitive traditions of its own" (Tetlow, 109). Analysts frequently divide the Gospel into "The Book of Signs" (1:19–12:50) and "The Book of Glory" (13:1–20:31), with a prologue and an epilogue. Tetlow points out that of the seven miraculous signs of Jesus' glory in the first section, the first and the last (at the marriage at Cana and the raising of Lazarus) include women (110).

> Now a certain man was ill, Lazarus, of Bethany, the village of
> Mary and her sister Martha. It was Mary who anointed the Lord
> with ointment and wiped his feet with her hair, whose brother
> Lazarus was ill. So the sisters sent to him, saying, "Lord, he
> whom you love is ill." But when Jesus heard it, he said, "This
> illness is not unto death; it is for the glory of God, so that the
> Son of God may be glorified by means of it." Now Jesus loved
> Martha and her sister and Lazarus. So when he heard that he
> was ill, he stayed two days longer in the place where he was.
> (John 11:1-6)

When Jesus arrives, Lazarus has already been four days in
the tomb. Martha goes out to meet him while Mary remains
at home. In the ensuing conversation, Jesus tells Martha that
"I am the resurrection and the life; he who believes in me,
though he die, yet shall he live, and whoever lives and believes in me shall never die. Do you believe this?" (John
11:25-26). Martha confesses: "Yes, Lord; I believe that you are
the Christ, the Son of God, he who is coming into the world"
(v. 27). The importance of this confession is underscored by
Tetlow:

> In the synoptic gospels the confession scene [of Peter at Caesarea
> Philippi] serves to underscore the primacy of Peter in apostolic
> authority. The gospel of John begins and ends with the procla-
> mation of Jesus as the Messiah and the Son of God. The sol-
> emn confession of Martha that Jesus is Messiah and Son of God
> is the climactic midpoint of the gospel. In this scene the most
> important role of discipleship according to johannine theology,
> that of proclamation of Jesus' true identity, is given to a woman.
> Since the fourth gospel was written on two levels, that of the
> time of the historical Jesus and that of the time of the johan-
> nine community, Martha is thus also portrayed by the evan-
> gelist as a focal point of apostolic authority in the johannine
> community (112).

After Martha's confession, she goes immediately to call her
sister Mary to come to Jesus. Tetlow sees this action as re-
flecting the "literary structure of the call narratives in John 1,
where, after Andrew believed, he immediately went and called

Simon Peter to come to Jesus. . . . In the fourth gospel literary structure is a theological tool of the evangelist. Here it serves to affirm the discipleship of Martha'' (112).

In verses 38–42, Jesus goes to the tomb, a cave with a stone placed against it, and commands those gathered to remove the stone. Martha, still the pragmatic one, speaks aloud her fear that the four-day-old corpse will stink. Jesus reminds her of her confession: ''Did I not tell you that if you would believe you would see the glory of God?'' The stone is removed, Jesus says ''Lazarus, come out''; the dead man comes forth, ''his hands and feet bound with bandages [translated as 'swathed in linen bands' in *The New English Bible*], his face wrapped with a cloth,'' and Jesus says ''Unbind him, and let him go'' (11:43-44).

From these happenings, I draw a picture of Martha's final conversion: when the stone is lifted, she too is loosed to live fully. William Temple, in *Readings in St. John's Gospel*, sees the stone as ''the stone which shuts the soul in its tomb of anxiety, or worry, or resentment. It involves the exposure of habits grown horrible in their rigidity. But it is the condition of response to the quickening voice'' (184). It is as though with one great breath, Martha also is brought to life; she accepts the miracle and crosses the threshold into the Household Jesus has prepared for her. She brings to fruition the ancient mysteries of weaving by accepting this initiation and rebirth Jesus offers.

To extend and deepen the message I felt Martha gave to me (to us) in this occasion, I wrote this dialogue:

> Nancy: Dear faithful Martha, how I see your qualities shining here! Jesus took the risk to cross out of safe territory back into Judea where enemies waited to kill him, and *you*, not thinking of danger but only of greeting your beloved friend, came to meet him. In this moment, Mary's staying seated in the house seems wrong—as though she is asleep and you are wide awake, ready to join with Jesus in a momentous time.
>
> Martha: Don't be too hard on Mary; she was overcome

by grief. And I, well, the only way I could deal with Lazarus' death was by keeping busy. When I heard Jesus was
coming I *had* to go out to him. I'll admit I felt both glad
to see him and disappointed—that's why I nearly scolded
him for not being here to save our brother.

Nancy: Yet you *acted*, you showed him your trust and
friendship, your unfailing hospitality (which he as un-
failingly reciprocated). You showed in your actions that
you understood the parable of the good shepherd, and
you fully accepted Jesus' message—the very message the
Jews had just been berating him for not plainly telling
them.

I see you being the sheep whom Jesus has called by
name, who knows his voice and follows him; I also see
you as the door-keeper, the one who recognizes the good
shepherd and ushers him in to gather his flock and to
lead them.

Martha: Yes, he wondrously enables me to find my very
centered place in his Household; I joyously serve as his
door-keeper—you remember that some have portrayed
me with keys to the Household, a bit like Peter's keys
to the Kingdom? What I find so amazing is that he called
me before ("Martha, Martha, . . . [only] one thing is needful" Luke 10:41-42), and I had so much to learn before I
could peacefully accept my own temperament and my
own gifts as fitting within his Household. Now he sees
that I am ready to take this enormous step with him and
he uses *exactly who I am* to announce his glory! Pragmatic,
busy, conscientious-to-a-fault, brusque me!

Nancy: That is what I so admire and love about you in
this passage. You and Mary both greet Jesus with the
same words (as John tells it): "If you had been here, my
brother would not have died!" But whereas Mary stops
with that and dissolves again into weeping at Jesus' feet,
you knew to move from regret in the past into present
and future hope: "And even now," you said, standing

ready beside him, "I know that whatever you ask from God, God will give you."

Martha: I had known his power, but not the full extent of his glory until he met me so directly. When I assured him I believed in the final resurrection, he pressed beyond that to a vision that took my breath away: he showed me that he gives eternal life *now*, and I had the wit (what a grace!) to blurt out what I suddenly knew: You are the Christ, the Son of God!

Nancy: Martha! Your action took you to him; your tenacity in loving attention to his Word enabled you to receive his central truth. And then, without hesitating, you went to share it with Mary, so that she too might be awakened and consoled.

Martha: I knew he would not leave me or Mary or the others alone, frozen in mourning. I had a premonition that he had risked his life coming here for something very important. He again is teaching me about "the one thing necessary"—in a stunning revelation I see that he will give his sheep eternal life, not just at the final resurrection, but *now*.

Satisfied that I *know*, he lets me serve as his intermediary in telling Mary and the others, and then at the tomb I help him announce it publicly. My blunt statement that the corpse would stink after its four days' interment removed any doubt that Lazarus was really dead—people thought that the soul lingered near the body for three days and then left. When Jesus replies, "Did I not tell you that if you have faith you will see the glory of God?" he is not rebuking me; he is speaking through me to all present, as he is when he prays to God for the sake of the people gathered there. Have no mistake, we are saying: this is no work of magic, it is a miracle and a revelation given to us by God through his Son!

Nancy: So you were not surprised when your brother emerged?

Martha: It was the greatest surprise of my life! That he would live a while longer in the flesh *and* that he would bear God's message that we who believe will live in spirit forever! When Jesus said "Unbind him, and let him go," I felt all *my* bindings of doubt and hesitation unravel, once and for all! Everything that I was and sometimes resented—my forwardness, my always "seeing things to do," my earthy pragmatism, my urges always to *act* upon life's stage—all these he used to show forth his most glorious message—He is Christ and his loving power cannot be overcome by death!

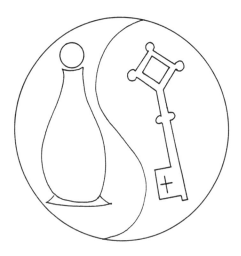

B. Mary's Pattern Flowers

The Book of Signs concludes in the next chapter of John (chapter 12), with the anointing of the feet of Jesus by Mary six days before the Passover festival in the house "where Lazarus was" [*The New English Bible* reads "lives"] in Bethany. "There they made him a supper; Martha served, and Lazarus was one of those at table with him" (12:2).

Brown finds the fact that Martha *served* at table significant: "The Evangelist is writing in the 90s, when the office of *diakonos* already existed in the post-Pauline churches (see the Pastorals) and when the task of waiting on tables was a specific function to which the community or its leaders appointed individuals by laying on hands (Acts 6:1-6)," i.e., Martha was exercising the function of an "ordained" person (690–91). For Tetlow, "The scene suggests eucharistic overtones since the context was set on Sunday, the day of eucharistic celebration in the johannine community. It is noteworthy that the ministers at the meal were both women" (113).

> Mary took a pound of costly ointment of pure nard and anointed the feet of Jesus and wiped his feet with her hair; and the house was filled with the fragrance of the ointment. But Judas Iscariot, one of his disciples (he who was to betray him) said, "Why was this ointment not sold for three hundred denarii and given to the poor?" This he said, not that he cared for the poor but because he was a thief, and as he had the money box he used to take what was put into it. Jesus said, "Let her alone, let her keep it for the day of my burial. The poor you always have with you, but you do not always have me" (John 12:3-8).

According to the *New Catholic Encyclopedia* commentary,

> Mary of Bethany (not to be confused with either Mary Magdalene or the penitent of Luke ch. 7), because of her deep, intuitive knowledge of Jesus' mystery, brought her discipleship to its perfection by anointing Jesus for His burial. Although she may not have been fully aware of the mystery of His death, through her one active service for Him, she has been reported in gospel history as the only one of all His disciples who, in some way, knew of His salvific death before it happened (Mark 14:6-9).

The weft leaps out in brilliant colors when this story enters our weaving. It is a tale of deep compassion revealing itself in a daring and creative act. Mary performs the first act of anointing Jesus, "which brought about immediate scandal"— her loose hair would have been grounds for mandatory divorce had she been married; a woman's hair was never to be uncovered in public (and if it was, she was most certainly a prostitute) (Ide, 39).

By Jesus' defense, we see that Mary is portrayed by the fourth evangelist as more truly a disciple than Judas.

> In the following chapter [of the Gospel of John] (13) the Book of Glory opens with the scene in which Jesus washes the disciples' feet. Here too the faithful ministry of Jesus is contrasted with the infidelity of Judas. Thus the ministry of Mary is shown to be authentic because it parallels the ministry of Jesus. This becomes explicit in 13:12-17. Jesus is portrayed explaining the nature of ministry and using the image of servant:
>
> > If I then, your Lord and Teacher, have washed your feet, you also ought to wash one another's feet.
>
> For I have given you an example, that you also should do as I have done to you (13:14-15). The importance of the example of Mary, who anticipated and fulfilled the authentic mode of ministry of the true disciple of Jesus, is highlighted by its structural position, bridging the two halves of the gospel (Tetlow, 113).

To fathom in my own way the revolutionary and creative act Mary has performed, I listen for Mary's voice and I write a dialogue in my journal with her:

Nancy: Mary, how did you conceive of doing what you did?

Mary: I just knew; I've never had such a friend. I feel what I did was for me and all of us. He allowed me to offer this gift; he accepted it and with it, all of me. He lets me be *all* that I ever would be and more, much more. Nothing I could give him would be too much.

Nancy: Weren't you embarrassed to show so intimately, in public, your love? And isn't that expensive oil a bit extravagant?

Mary: Oh, no! With him I never care what is "proper"; somehow he frees me from that. I felt I had to touch him in the most loving, lavish way I could afford—to prepare for whatever had to come.

Nancy: I *do* feel as though you've done this for *me* also, and I thank you. But this fragrance reminds me of death as well as of joy; it makes me feel fear.

Mary: Oh yes, I know that—I tried to bring joy out of my own fear and impending sadness, to give him what pleasure I could. I can't quite bring myself to believe he will really leave us.

Nancy: I've heard of an apocryphal saying of Jesus, "Whosoever is near to me is near to the fire"—does that make sense to you now, Mary?

Mary: Yes—so much that it gives me shivers. He is the hearth/heart of our household, our beloved Friend, the one whose warmth feeds our deepest hungers; yet in these moments I feel the flame leaping up. It somehow portends his suffering. All I can do is offer this anointing as my way of telling him I love him and will go with him even through the fire.

Nancy: What about Judas' rebuke and Jesus' answer? Why *didn't* you give this to the poor?

Mary: For this moment I saw what he needed (or rather what *I* needed to give him; what I alone knew how to give) and so I gave. I thought of David's dancing before the Ark as I performed my "dance" at his feet; I felt that kind of holy joy. Through him I know what and why and how to give to the poor—it's not an either/or in my life. He is simply *first* for me, and I have the incredible privilege to serve him with what I have, right now.

Mary transforms a servile task, washing the feet of the master, and using her hair to wipe them clean, into an act which signifies her own transformation. She has found her unique way of showing her love to her lord and teacher. We can only imagine what the others thought. Was Martha shocked and then amazed at her sister's daring? And Jesus, what a surprise and a frankly sensual delight she gives him; what a reassurance that his teaching has taken firm hold in her spirit. As she courageously responds to his courage, to his love, she flowers fully into a maturity of her own.

The fact that "the house was filled with the fragrance of the ointment" also suggests the permeation of the "house spirit" with the outpouring love of her deed. Like ascending incense, this fragrance signifies the presence of the spirit of holiness, and as each person present breathes it, he or she shares in it (cf. Psalm 141:2: "Let my prayer be counted as incense before thee, and the lifting up of my hands as an evening sacrifice!").

I recall that J. E. Cirlot in *A Dictionary of Symbols* mentions a richly evocative relation between hair and thread: "According to the Zohar [a Jewish mystical commentary on the Pentateuch], thread is one of the most ancient of symbols (like hair). It denotes the essential connection between any of the different planes—the spiritual, biological, social, etc." (323). Thus I see Mary's anointment of Jesus' feet as weaving together all the worlds Christ himself weaves together in his being.

MARY ANOINTS JESUS' FEET

What men think!
Unbinding my hair,
I am disgraced in their eyes.
Unbinding my hair,
I feel grace in your gaze.

As this oil epitomizes
earth's riches,
its fragrance ascending to heaven,
so you, my Friend,
are my life's treasure,
so your royal spirit lifts me up.

If I can afford your being
pleasure and honor,
no risk is too great—
you have taught me that,
and it has set me free.

As I kneel at your feet,
I receive your blessing;
as I anoint you with this oil,
it becomes a river
of your love.

Though you suffer a
cross of fire,
give me courage to be with you.
The waters of paradise
heal all wounds.

(Nancy Corson Carter, in *Womenpsalms* [Winona, Minn.: St. Mary's Press, 1992])

I find that in the Gospel of John, both Martha and Mary reach particular fulfillment in their lives, their ministries. I look again at Martha's comment that Lazarus' corpse will stink, at her concern with the bodily needs of her family and guests, and I think of her as the sensual, earthy counterpart to the more intuitive, ethereal Mary. Her usually very practical, physical fact-oriented self is the necessary complement to Mary's usually impractical, spiritually-oriented self. In the John stories, it is as though both are enabled, through Jesus' guiding presence, to become complete.

In one way of speaking of the power of Jesus' incarnation (I am influenced here by Joseph Campbell's discussion in "Love and the Goddess," part of the TV interview series, *The Power of Myth*, he did with Bill Moyers), Jesus represents the golden embrace of heaven and earth in our heart/compassion center. Martha as "earth" receives the gift of "heaven" when she recognizes Jesus as the Christ who brings eternal life. Likewise, Mary as "heaven" incorporates "earth" in her wondrously sensual act of anointing Jesus.

For Martha and Mary, the "way" is toward completion and fulfillment. They must find the path of discipleship that for each of them is their unique way to serve God single-heartedly, to shed anxiety in living their lives centered on the "one thing necessary."

Working Through Anxieties to Affirmations

As I consider the kind of apotheosis, the kind of achievement of an ideal state that I have just described for both Martha and Mary, I realize that to end there would not be right. Both women undoubtedly had these wondrous "mountaintop" moments when they felt what Jesus meant for them in their discipleship. But like us, and we also have probably had moments when we glimpsed such fulfillment of our own discipleship, they had to continue their life's journey. They had yet to encounter Jesus' death and resurrection; they had yet to complete their divine/mundane life journeys. As they struggled to maintain their focus on "the one thing necessary," they surely felt moments of loss, confusion, and anxiety.

I thought of my own frequent need to re-focus on the great Center of my life. I overheard, in imagination, the voices of both Nancy-Martha and Nancy-Mary spelling out their woes over moments when they slipped away from the joy they had experienced in knowing themselves so directly centered in Christ's vision. Nancy-Martha has particular trouble remembering her own power to speak and to act; curiously she finds herself envying others for qualities and achievements that she has somehow forgotten she herself possesses. When she catches herself in such absurd entanglements she feels deep chagrin. She remembers the magnificent power Jesus showed her in her own forthright practicality that openly names Truth. Nancy-Mary becomes afraid of her own passionate nature and feels it becoming rigid and timid; she lets the wide expanse of the universe shrink to a little black box around her until somehow she lets herself respond to Jesus' voice calling her to come out.

In search of some more practical ways to keep myself less vulnerable to such unworthy anxieties, I recently re-read a chapter from Richard J. Foster's book, *Celebration of Discipline; The Path to Spiritual Growth*, called "The Discipline of Simplicity." In this chapter, Foster emphasizes that simplicity demands a focal point to keep it from being legalistic and self-serving. This focal point is found in Jesus' words in Matthew 6:25-33:

> Therefore I tell you, do not be anxious about your life, what you shall eat or what you shall drink, nor about your body, what you shall put on. Is not life more than food, and the body more than clothing? . . . Therefore do not be anxious, saying "What shall we eat?" or "What shall we drink?" or "What shall we wear?" For the Gentiles seek all these things; and your heavenly Father knows that you need them all. *But seek first his kingdom and his righteousness, and all these things shall be yours as well.*

"The person who does not seek the kingdom first," writes Foster, "does not seek it at all, regardless of how worthy the idolatry that he or she has substituted for it" (76). Framed so, the lesson that Martha is being encouraged to learn in the setting of Luke 10:38-42 is this: even a well-meant service may become idolatrous when we forget, even momentarily, that the one thing, the first thing, is to seek God's Household (I've substituted this word for "kingdom"). In terms of our weaving, God's Household as revealed in the Word is our warp—if we give it primary attention as we weft on threads, we weave solidly and well; if we forget and weave distractedly, fretfully, we let our tensions wreck the balanced evenness of the work, resulting in unsightly and weakened fabric.

Pointing to Matthew 6:25-33, Foster underlines Jesus' clear statement that freedom from anxiety is one of the inward evidences of seeking the Household of God first (76). He goes on to discuss three inner attitudes that characterize freedom from anxiety: (1) gratitude to God for all that we have; (2) trust in God to care for what he has given us, not only our possessions but such things as our reputation and our employment; (3) generosity—making our goods, our talents, our service freely available to others (77–78).

Let me weave one more passage, Matthew 11:28-30, into our fabric about service: "Come to me, all who labor and are heavy laden, and I will give you rest. Take my yoke upon you, and learn from me; for I am gentle and lowly in heart, and you will find rest for your souls. For my yoke is easy, and my burden is light."

Pondering again what lesson Jesus offers Martha and each of us as he asks us not to be troubled and distracted, but to choose instead the "one thing necessary," I see that we are given an easy indicator to tell us how we are doing. When we find ourselves anxious and troubled, we must stop and consider how to let go of this burden, how to lift it up and be rested. If we are tense and over-stressed, it is a message that we are allowing ourselves to grind into what a friend calls "fifth gear over-Martha." In this state we are trying to use energy that we simply cannot generate from ourselves alone; having used up our supply, we rev wildly, disconnectedly; at the loom we strain and pull at the threads until they are ready to snap.

Depending upon our own temperament and situation, we may need to go on retreat, for an hour, a day, or a week, and deeply center down so that our service may be re-centered in the Household; or, if we do not have the time or inclination for this, if we are well enough disciplined, we may need simply to catch ourselves in our distracted state and say a prayer such as this while we work: "Lord, be present in what I do; let me know it is your yoke I choose to wear, that it is easy and full of light."

A short poem-meditation on smiling by Thich Nhat Hanh, a Vietnamese Buddhist monk, gives us another perspective on how we may become present and peaceful. We cannot imagine Martha smiling as she complained to Jesus. Can we imagine ourselves smiling when *we* are stressed out?

Thich Nhat Hanh reminds us that "a smile can relax hundreds of muscles in your face, and relax your nervous system. A smile makes you master of yourself" (6). So he offers these helpful words for us to recite while we breathe and smile:

"Breathing in, I calm my body.
Breathing out, I smile.
Dwelling in the present moment
I know this is a wonderful moment" (5).

When we ask our Lord to be present, it might be very wonderful if we would smile!

Affirmations

Since the time we worked with affirmations on a women's retreat, I and my fellow retreatants have found how empowering they can be in dealing with our anxieties. Following the formula for an affirmation as my friend, Elizabeth Hinton, and others have developed it for use in spiritual growth, we practiced stating the goals we had for ourselves in our lives as though we had already achieved them. For example, one of my friends said she had been amazed at how simply stating to herself, "I, Nan, am calm and centered," had helped her deal with some extremely frustrating events during a workshop she gave the week after the retreat.

Naturally, using affirmations entails a nice balancing of idealism and realism. From one perspective, the affirmations could be viewed as a form of "as-if" psychology: we affirm something we hope to attain in our lives as if we already have received it. On the other hand, this is a form of prayer: we tell God what our most treasured goals are and ask for guidance in achieving them. This is a way to test our sense of limits, our sense of just how many gifts and how much abundance we can accept as God's children; it is also a way to practice "thy will be done" if in fact we come to see that we have selected inappropriate goals. Then we must have the wisdom to either modify or change them.

I am using an affirmation to keep from the ego-bugged, too-busy procrastinator-distractors as I juggle my teaching and housewifing with this writing; I keep on my desk and repeat daily this affirmation: "I, Nancy, with the guidance of the Spirit, am joyfully writing a soon-to-be-published book about Martha, Mary, and Jesus." And I am allowing it to work, with Spirit's guidance, in my life, especially since I wisely decided to let God determine what "soon" means! I have an "escape clause" (which I will accept only reluctantly, I admit) that this

goal may not be in God's will; but for now, I feel that this is
an appropriate affirmation for me. It helps dispel anxiety and
frees me to concentrate upon this work as centered in "the
one thing necessary."

If you would like to use affirmations as a tool for centering
your own life and service, look over the following guidelines
which I have paraphrased from Elizabeth Hinton.

Basic How To's of Affirmations:

1. Make them in short, positive statements.
2. Use present tense verbs only (no "will" verbs; no "I
hope" statements).
3. Put your name in each time you say, think, or write
them. Put your name in each one, each time.
4. Write them with no frills and then write them with
strong emotional words like joyfully, gleefully, happily,
easily, effortlessly, lovingly, completely, wholly, etc. If
these words elicit an argument or a strong response from
you, keep them in the affirmation (they may indicate your
own place of stubborn will-to-be-distracted).
5. Read the affirmations at least once a day, preferably
twice.
6. Write them at least once a day, if you want to see faster
results. Try different ways of putting your affirmations
in your day. Carry them around on cards, on a tape
recording, in pictures. Repeat them at meals, while you
are driving, or doing repetitious work or waiting, or while
you are exercising.
7. Know that God will be your partner and helpmate if
you ask. Ask for the Spirit to support you and to continue to give you courage to *know* these affirmations are
real and true.

(Rules above used with Elizabeth G. Hinton's permission,
from her newsletter *Unfolding* 1:4 [9 September 1984].)

Here are some affirmation suggestions:

I, _____ (fill in your name), trust myself and my affirmations.

I, _____, trust God to heal me and to guide my life-weaving.

I, _____, am calm and centered in "the one thing necessary."

I, _____, am able to deal with (name your own most troublesome distraction) today in a calm and loving way.

I, _____, am able to turn crises into opportunities to serve God more fully.

I, _____, know God is with me always.

What I know for myself is that these affirmations are really a form of prayer, a prayer which trusts God's leading me beyond my distractions to a fuller and more joyful service. A biblical text I keep before me as I open myself to learning how better to serve is Philippians 4:6-7: "Have no anxiety about anything, but in everything by prayer and supplication with thanksgiving let your requests be made known to God. And the peace of God, which passes all understanding, will keep your hearts and your minds in Christ Jesus."

Chapter 7

Prayer as Context:
Text and Textile as One

For the contemplative, the way of discovering meaning is to discover how to be of service, and the way toward service is through surrender (Gerald G. May, *Will and Spirit: A Contemplative Psychology,* 208).

To end this weaving in fullness, to give it a border that most allows the kind of ongoing birthing/weaving of the self-in-Household I sought in the beginning, I turn to prayer. What could more powerfully aid in making a transition from that ego-centered time of life I felt was ending toward what I anticipated as a time of putting myself in the service of a larger, transpersonal realm? What could more directly weave together the worlds I sought to reconcile, Mary's "text"/study and contemplation and Martha's "textile"/action? How also to deal with the difficulties that appear even in the most well-established service—I am constantly reminded that I will never be totally free of pettiness, jealousy, and wrong-headedness in my discipleship. At such moments of disappointment, my only true resource is in praying that I be forgiven and restored to "the joy of your salvation."

It seems especially right in the Light of this weaving that the story of Martha and Mary receiving Jesus into their home appears in Luke at the end of chapter 10, immediately before

Luke's account of Jesus' teaching his disciples how to pray: "He was praying in a certain place, and when he ceased, one of his disciples said to him, 'Lord, teach us to pray, as John taught his disciples.' And he said to them, 'When you pray, say:

'Father, hallowed be thy name. Thy kingdom come. Give us each day our daily bread, and forgive us our sins, for we ourselves forgive every one who is indebted to us; and lead us not into temptation' '' (Luke 11:1-4).

The gospel writers frequently mention Jesus' setting aside time for prayer. Matthew and Mark tell of his going "up into the hills by himself to pray" after feeding the five thousand (Matthew 14:23; Mark 6:46); Luke writes (6:12) that "In these days he went out into the hills to pray; and all night he continued in prayer to God." He also teaches his disciples to pray; he sometimes takes them with him as when Peter, James, and John accompany him into the mountains to pray and are present at his transfiguration; he asks his disciples to stay and pray with him at Gethsemane; we know his poignant prayers of forgiveness and acceptance at Golgotha.

We also see how integrally related Jesus understands prayer and healing to be. In Mark 9:25-29, for example, when his disciples ask why they could not cast out the evil spirit from an epileptic boy, Jesus answers (v. 29): "This kind cannot be driven out by anything but prayer." Prayer is to be their ultimate discipline, their basic way of opening to God's great healing power for themselves and for others.

In John (17:9-26) we read of Jesus' continual praying for his disciples: "Holy Father, keep them in thy name, which thou hast given me, that they may be one, even as we are one" (v. 11); the passage concludes: "I made known to them thy name, and I will make it known, that the love with which thou hast loved me may be in them, and I in them."

Before Jesus calls Martha's and Mary's brother Lazarus back to life after the tomb stone has been removed, he looks upward and prays this prayer (John 11:41b-42): "Father, I thank thee that thou hast heard me. I knew that thou hearest me al-

ways, but I have said this on account of the people standing
by that they might believe that thou didst send me." William
Temple's commentary reminds us of the constancy of Jesus'
prayer: "There was no one moment of prayer; He lived in
prayer, and doubtless was in prayer from the time when the
message of the sisters reached Him. Now for a moment He
reveals His prayer and His assurance that it is answered" (184).

If Jesus knew that he must keep in loving communication
with God through prayer, how much more *we* need to do that!
I think of Mary's being quietly at Jesus' feet and of Martha's
fidgeting about her work; I remember a line from Psalm 46:
"Be still and know that I am God," and see that Mary's inner
and outer presence manifest this stillness. Certainly that still,
attentive waiting upon God is the attitude of prayer.

That still attentiveness seems so much to me like weaving—
it suggests a patient, skillful work that attunes the weaver to
rhythms that are universal, like those of breath and blood and
sea and air, to rhythms that produce health and wholeness (a
"bodymindspirit endorphin" activity!).

Prayer Situates Our Work in Space and Time

Previously, I referred to the Tedlocks' article about the
weaving of the Quiché Maya. In it, they describe the role of
prayer in a way that enlarges this theme of attunement:
Weavers pray before they begin work, invoking both celestial
and earthly deities and explicitly situating their work within
the *cal xucut caj, caj xucut ulew*, "four corners of the sky, four
corners of earth" (129).

For the Quiché Maya as for us, prayer is a situating of our
work. Perhaps there really is no other way than to begin with
prayer, whether we mean a day, a specific project, or a life,
and to stay in prayer as we breathe, as we weave. We ask
Christ to be our intermediary between the realms of heaven
and earth, we ask him to be the shuttle, the priest who joins
these spaces into one great temple. (Note that the Latin word
for "priest" is *pontifex*, from *pons*, "bridge" and *facio*, "to

make"; thus we may construct a multi-layered metaphor of priestly woven bridges!)

If we pray before we work, we open our work to transformation, toward a larger use in the Household of God. As the prayer we pray before sleep enters into us and breathes us all through the night, so the prayer before work enters into us and breathes/weaves us and our work, connecting our own humble microcosmic household with the heavenly macrocosmic Household.

A woman who attended a Catholic grade school spoke of how she and all the other children were required to physically lift up to God their books, their paper and pencils, or whatever they were working with, each hour when the clock struck. I am led by that image to images of the bells which rang from the great European cathedrals in a time when everyone hearing them remembered that God is both in and out of time, that God is with us always if we would only notice this and praise its being so. I am learning to re-tune my ears to this message of bells, wherever I hear them ring.

As the gothic cathedrals are oriented with apse and altar in the East where the Sun/Son rises, so by prayer we orient our work within our domestic space analogously with sacred space. As Christ embodies the great mystery of God incarnate, so our breathing-weaving, praying-acting makes an interpenetrating fabric of time and space. From one of our Jewish midrashim, I remember a phrase: "The temple is in space what the sabbath is in time."

What we are intentionally weaving is an openness to the interpenetration of mystery, a way to realize as sacred the mundane worlds of space and time. Prayer is our invitation to the Holy Spirit to enter in and make us more transparent, more penetrable. (I played with some word-threads from *penetrate* and found: the same Latin root for (a) *penetralia*—the innermost parts of a building, especially the sanctuary of a temple; innermost or hidden parts; recesses: *the penetralia of the soul* and (b) *penetrate*—to enter or force a way into; pierce; to grasp the inner significance of; to gain insight [into something].)

Evelyn Underhill synthesizes the spatial metaphor with the idea of prayer as a "combining power" for Mary and Martha in *The House of the Soul*: "The sense of cleavage between the duties of Mary and Martha, and a certain uneasy effort to combine them, is responsible for much psychic untidiness, tension and weakening fuss. When the whole house is devoted to one interest, and a working harmony is established between the upper and the lower floor, each action, however homely, has the quality of prayer; since every corner and all that is done in it is informed by God and tends to God" (46–47).

Thus Underhill reminds us again of Jesus' saying "In my Father's house are many mansions," and the repeated use in the New Testament of the metaphors of the household of God, the body of believers, and the body as a temple of the Holy Spirit.

Simone Weil once wrote, "Absolute attention is prayer." For me, prayer is attention to the "one thing necessary," an orientation which I received in baptism and to which I am being continuously converted if I will *only attend*.

One reason the weaving metaphor holds such appeal for me is that if I image my life as the weft and God's Word as warp, then I understand that this warp holds me, gives me shape and meaning. The rhythmic over and under of the plain weave is a constant interrelating of my life with God's presence; as I breathe and weave, I am breathed and woven by God—it is a miraculously reciprocal creation-relationship. In this breathing-praying-weaving we co-create the miracle of incarnation (we might even coin the word "co-incarnation" to speak of it). In this praying, I more fully understand the reciprocity of the hospitality Martha and Jesus share, and, likewise, the anointing-blessing Mary and Jesus share.

Once, as I was pondering the meaning of prayer in this weaving, I took out my felt-tip pens and began to sketch a sort of "woven world" image of a tree with two red birds in it with blue sky and golden sun woven in and around its brown trunk and green leaves. I was using lines I meant to represent threads passing over and under each other at right angles to look like

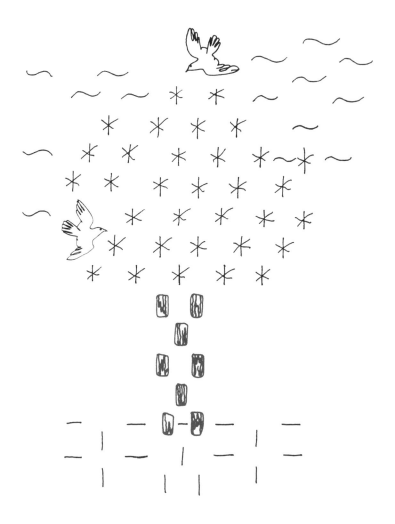

a plain weave sampler figure. As I sketched I was reminded of the notion from the new physics that we are not solid, that we are a great deal more penetrable and interpenetrating than we let on most of the time. The weaving image connected with a poem I had written entitled ''Lacemaker'' (Nancy Corson Carter, in *The Garfield Lake Review*, 1990):

Intent upon
her pillow of spool-weighted threads
she lets the sun dip down,
past clay chimneys,
below the dark swan mirrors
of Bruges canals.

The old lacemaker,
older than any of her sisters,
weaves the lineage of their desires,
their fruits and failures;
daughter of Arachne, of Penelope, of Mary,
she spins her web
with endless delicacy.

Though she is nearly blind
her fingers know by touch
the patterns of her trade:
among them Mechlin, Binche,
Brussels, the "belle et éternelle"
Valenciennes.

These patterns
epitomize mysteries:
filaments of light and water
enmeshing earth life,
wisdom passed from ancient times
through the wind-warped soil,
through generational networks
of nerve and sinew
into the blood singing
in her capillary threads.

No matter that the sinking sun
takes the little light she had;
behind her eyes other eyes open;
they see what her fingers
encode in snowy lace:
the pattern that connects it all.

So many of the crafts of fabric making are contemplative in nature; full of repetitions and tediousness, they require a similar solitary stillness and concentration. What I imagine as the lacemaker's "dawning in darkness" insight is that our pattern-making, plumbed to its depths, reveals its always-present but seldom recognized connection with Pattern, another way of naming God as source of our own making.

Those craftspersons who perform "women's work" to provide lovely things for the rich often do so at real cost to themselves, not only monetarily, but also physically. Likewise, prayer is a sacrifice we make for the loveliness of the Household, a steadfast weaving of a fabric full of love, humility, and mystery.

Breathing/Weaving

Once again I become aware of the analogies between breathing and weaving; our breath is the in-and-out weaving of life in us. When we consciously focus on our breath in what some call the "breath prayer," we remind ourselves of this. In the breath prayer we allow one devotional phrase, whether it be the ancient Jesus Prayer, "Lord Jesus Christ, have mercy on me, a sinner" or another phrase of our own choice (often simply the name of God which has most power for us) to be repeated over and over in rhythm with our breathing, our life-functioning, to breathe and be breathed by it into deeper relationship with the "still small voice" of God.

The breath prayer makes us attentive to the fundamental pattern, our inspiration-expiration rhythms of life-death interwoven. Every breath thus considered is a breath of Life, and every crossing over and under the warp is a wefting embrace of the Word. When we breathe fully and faithfully, we are performing an anti-anxiety, anti-fear act in the world; such breath is the opposite of hyperventilation or asphyxiation—it gives us centered life instead of scattering threats of death. In this breath we exercise our full response-ability toward the informing breath of Spirit.

Such a breathing-weaving concentrates and opens us, widens us beyond our individual ego bounds into the "more" that is God; it has to do, I am sure, with the kind of "emptying out" (Greek *kenosis*) which Jesus was able to do (see Philippians 2:5-7—"Have this mind among yourselves, which you have in Christ Jesus, who, though he was in the form of God, did not count equality with God a thing to be grasped, but emptied himself, taking the form of a servant, being born in the likeness of men").

Penance and Pausing

I must be careful, though, not to be caught in the practice of weaving for its own sake, being so busy, even about my "contemplative work," that I do not really become still. I am learning that if, in my writing and in my teaching, I am to be an enabler of others' prayer and contemplation, I must be careful to maintain my own through daily discipline. For example, after helping to lead a women's retreat I wrote in my journal:

> In order to *lead* a retreat, you really need to be in "Martha mode" as an enabler of others' "Mary mode." What is true for me I believe must also be true for others, including Jesus: you must balance out "Martha mode" teaching, leading, and working times with "Mary mode" times. Jesus often withdrew into quiet places where he could be alone to pray. So too, I see it is imperative for me to place "Martha mode" time within a matrix of "Mary mode" time. I did this partially by saying sacrament of penance with Father Lawson before leaving for our retreat. I have had trouble really nurturing my Mary self since I returned because I have had to plunge right back into teaching courses, catching up on housework, etc., and it's been hard for me not to feel distracted, at least from my "Mary work."

I notice several things about this entry as I write it out again: I seem to have a temperamental resistance to pulling that thread of "Maryness" through my "Marthaness"; I hope I will not always so automatically separate them. Despite the great benefits of the balance, I still have periods of relapse when I am a terribly unclear Martha. On the other hand, I notice that I do take the time to sit down and write in the journal, often an entryway into contemplation for me.

Another thing I notice in this entry is my recognition of the importance of penance as a preparation for work intentionally open to Spirit's leading. Since I have belonged to churches of the Protestant tradition from the time I was baptized as an infant, penance is not a sacrament familiar to me. I had said confession only in a public worship setting. But Father Lawson's gentle persuasion led me to acknowledge the importance of personal confession and absolution.

Søren Kierkegaard's *Purity of Heart is to Will One Thing: Spiritual Preparation for the Office of Confession* helped me understand more about this sacrament. From it I copied down this wonderful wisdom about prayer: "The prayer does not change God, but it changes the one who offers it" (51). Further, I was drawn to his description of confession as a stay against distraction: "For confession is a holy act, which calls for a collected mind. A collected mind is a mind that has collected itself from every distraction, from every relation, in order to center itself upon this relation to itself as an individual who is responsible to God" (215).

Saying the sacrament of penance before going on retreat helped me unburden much ego-baggage. I knew that my two co-leaders and I could not really work the wonder of community and growth which we intended without a ready openness to Spirit.

Penance, in fact, as Kierkegaard says, *collects* us and helps us put any and all of our important charges in God's hands. If you are as vulnerable as I am to getting into "fifth gear over-Martha" in your projects, I can recommend saying penance and receiving absolution as a way to remember that God will be present in all we do if we but ask.

Kierkegaard's advocacy of *pausing* also struck me with its

relevance to our efforts in balancing Martha and Mary in our lives (I trust he would have used inclusive language if he were writing today):

> But what does it profit a man if he goes further and further and it must be said of him: he never stops going further; when it also must be said of him: there was nothing that made him pause? For pausing is not a sluggish repose. Pausing is also movement. It is the inward movement of the heart. To pause is to deepen oneself in inwardness. But merely going further is to go straight in the direction of superficiality. By that way one does not come to will only one thing. Only if at some time he decisively stopped going further and then again came to a pause, as he went further, only then could he will only one thing. For purity of heart is to will one thing (217–18).

Kierkegaard's meditation is based on James 4:8: ''Draw near to God and he will draw near to you. Cleanse your hands, you sinners, and purify your hearts, you men of double mind.'' It seems to me that through what I have called my ''Mary mode,'' I learn in stillness what it means to confess, to receive the purification of absolution and then to rise up and be in ''Martha mode'' in a whole new single-minded, freely joyful way.

The links between prayer and penance and pausing are extremely important for me to continue to recognize. When I went on sabbatical a year ago, I knew I was entering into a kind of Great Pause of many activities I had come to depend upon for self-importance. I was in one of my ambivalent states about all my busy Martha projects—at the church alone there was my status as active elder, my involvement with the women's retreat group, and the environmental group to let go. As I moved away, literally and figuratively, for a year, I felt relief to be unburdened of these responsibilities *and* anxiety about losing my ''place.'' As I look back, I am grateful that I renewed my efforts to be disciplined in contemplation and prayer during the sabbatical. My initially unseen needs were to submit to change, to let the Spirit reshape me in yet-unknown ways. Parker Palmer defines ''contemplation'' in a way that matches the dynamic I experienced: "I understand contemplation to be any way that we can unveil the illusions that masquerade as reality and reveal the reality behind the masks" (*The Active Life*, 17).

In prayer/penance/pausing I learn and re-learn my need to strip away the countless masks that I tend to wear long beyond their usefulness. As I went on sabbatical, I was turning from an emphasis on my Martha self to an emphasis on my Mary self. Although I was eager to spend time in quiet study and meditation, I needed help to make a transition, to see how I could stay centered on "the one thing necessary" in a different environment. When I returned from the sabbatical I had need to submit again to the unmasking; I feared that other persons had "taken my place," and I needed strengthening to see how I could newly serve.

Emptying (*Kenosis*)

There are several more threads I want to draw across the loom in this consideration of prayer and contemplation. One of them continues the theme of emptying or *kenosis*. As I ponder and research this Martha and Mary weaving, I often receive timely "shipments of yarn"; one such "shipment" was a copy of *A Letter of Private Direction* by the author of the *Cloud of Unknowing*. In it, I read:

> Make sure that your contemplation is not divided and that your love is pure. Make sure that you are like that, so that you yourself, and nothing else at all, are worked on by grace and quietly nourished in your will to love God alone—God just as God is. Don't forget that union with God will be unseeing and imperfect (for that is the only way it can be in this mortal life), and in that way keep your longing to be with God lively and ardent.
>
> So look up! Be joyful and say to your Lord (aloud or inside yourself): "Lord, I offer you whatever I am, for you are what I am." Then concentrate very hard, and think quite plainly and with all your force, just that you are as you are—but don't start

worrying your mind about this in any way, just think it. You don't have to be an expert to think like this (22).

It is particularly this prayer that captures me: "Lord, I offer you whatever I am, for you are what I am." When I read these words, I recognize a message meant for me. When I said the words in meditation the day after I had first focused upon them, I experienced a great sense of release—it was as though tightness and tension which blocked the flow of energy in my system now opened and allowed me to become a part of a great exchange of energy with the God who surrounds me always. This healing, comforting, wholly accepting Presence so "unbound" me that happy tears streamed down my face.

This seems a dilemma which afflicts nearly all of us: we live in a world of Martha and we hunger and thirst for the world of Mary to be ours as well. Evelyn Underhill underscores this perception in one of her *Twelve Essays and Addresses:*

> We may speak respectfully of Mary, and even study her psychology; but we feel that the really important thing is to encourage Martha to go on getting the lunch. Yet the whole witness of religious history supports St. Luke and Aristotle and St. Gregory. Understood in the deepest and widest sense, contemplation is the very life blood of religion. It is and has ever been the one thing needful, "the life of man most fully man." Be still and *know* that I am God. It cannot be done in any other way. It is true that he who runs may read; but he cannot so easily observe the stars.
>
> So here is something which the religious philosopher cannot neglect. It is his duty to heal the conflict between practical life and contemplative life. He must remind our institutional Marthas that the whole sanction for their activities—the only reason why religion exists at all—abides in the fact that men and women do possess a sense of God, of Eternal Life; that they are contemplative animals (5).

Yet I must remind myself, since I have a proclivity to favor Mary over Martha (philosophically, that is; practically, I tend to get lost in Martha work), that we are each called to honor

God in our lives in different ways. In the Catholic Church there are orders designated "contemplative," orders designated as "active," and still other "mixed" orders. The author of *A Letter of Private Direction* writes:

> That is my reading of the gospel statement: "You can't do anything without me." It is to be taken one way for those who live the active life and in another way for those who follow the contemplative life. God must necessarily be with those who live an active life, either by sufferance or by consent or by both, in everything they do, whether what they do is permissible and acceptable to him or not. He must necessarily be with those who lead a contemplative life, as its prime mover, demanding no more from them but to accept him and agree to whatever he does. All this means that we can't do anything without God, whatever we do, permissible or not, active or contemplative (60–61).

Jacques and Raissa Maritain in *Liturgy and Contemplation* write that "Those souls whose style of life is active will have the grace of contemplation; perhaps they will be capable only of reciting rosaries, and mental prayer will bring them only a headache or sleep. Mysterious contemplation will not be in their conscious prayer, but perhaps in the glance with which they will look at a poor man, or look at suffering" (36–37).

Thomas Merton writes in *What is Contemplation?* that there are many Christians of whom it might be said that "Although they are active laborers, they are also quasi-contemplatives because of the great purity of heart maintained in them by obedience, fraternal charity, self sacrifice and perfect abandonment to God's will in all that they do and suffer. They are much closer to God than they realize. They enjoy a kind of 'masked' contemplation" (14–15). Whatever our way is to be, active, contemplative, or mixed, we are to seek one thing alone continues Merton: "To purify your love of God more and more, to abandon yourself more and more perfectly to His will, and to love Him more exclusively and more completely, but also more simply and more peacefully and with more totally uncompromising trust" (25).

Another way of putting it, this thread of emptying oneself in order to be more lovingly obedient to God's will, no matter what our temperament, our "way," is this: we must seek to weave it truly, not in a false quietist or escapist way, but in a way that brings us into more profound contact with the world. Thus I am drawn to Gerald G. May's words as he speaks to contemplatives in his work *Will and Spirit: A Contemplative Psychology*: he notes that "For the contemplative, the way of discovering meaning is to discover how to be of service, and the way toward service is through surrender" (208). Furthermore, we who have this tendency toward the contemplative must undertake the difficult task of combining this surrender and service in our daily lives. This requires that we must, as May emphasizes, learn this principle: "To pray as if all depends on divine action is to support passivity and self-suppression. To labor as if all depended on our own effort is to court willfulness in a dangerous way. We are decidedly more talented at doing the latter than the former, yet it is *both* that are demanded if one's spiritual journey is to be meaningfully reflected in life" (208–209).

The Issachar and Zebulun Model

It becomes clear to me that when St. Teresa said "to give our Lord a perfect service, Martha and Mary must combine," she was exactly right (Underhill, *Twelve Essays*, 74). Yet in discerning just exactly *how* we are to do this combining, both interpersonally and intrapersonally, we are challenged to our depths. I have suggested in my journaling and poetry excerpts that my own primary approach to this challenge has been intrapersonal. Yet I am learning to expand my understanding into the interpersonal realm, where I feel it also belongs. I have been instructed by the Hasidic Issachar and Zebulun model and am now questioning how that model may indicate ways to communally combine Martha and Mary.

According to biblical-tribal tradition, Zebulun the merchant and Issachar the student of Torah contract to mutually support each other: "Issachar's actualization depends on his studying the Torah for himself and for Zebulun, independent of the latter's support or gratitude; Zebulun's salvation depends on his supporting Issachar, although the latter has no material debts in relation to the former" (Rotenberg, 20). According to Rabbi Yaacov Yosef, early Hasidic leaders emphasized that "it is functional for the salvation of the rich 'people of matter' to support the 'people of form' so they too will be uplifted and redeemed. Moreover, these early Hasidic leaders stressed that this system of mutual help is functional for the maintenance and survival of the entire community, as the 'people of form' have a moral influence on the 'people of matter,' and the latter reciprocate by bestowing material goodness upon the former" (Rotenberg, 24).

One of my Coolidge Colloquium colleagues told me that in Rabbinic Judaism (roughly contemporary with Jesus) there are some teachings in the Wisdom of the Fathers (*Pirke Avot*) that shed light upon this theme: study is equivalent to all the other *mitzvot* (commandments) because it leads to action; but it was considered that a life without labor was not a full life. In the *Pirke Avot* 2:2 it is written that "All torah study which is not combined with some trade must at length fail and occasion sin"!

It would seem that each of us must determine the Martha-Mary (analogous to the Zebulun-Issachar) balance within ourselves and between us and our community. We consider our talents, our particular personal/communal situations and need/desire incentives, and make the best choices we can. Of course, we can seldom settle these matters once and for all since, as individuals as well as communities, we have our fluctuating seasons of being more Martha or Mary. You and I, for example, as reader and writer, are probably in quite different relationships of Martha and Maryness, yet in both cases we may consider ourselves being in a mysterious balance of community as we seek "the one thing necessary."

I refer again to the images of temple and sabbath; I am reminded that both require the context of community. What temple serves only one person? What sabbath is properly celebrated for one alone? In time and space the temple and the sabbath are celebrations of the community of God seeing itself as a collection of individuals drawn together into one body in worship. Even in our greatest moments of loneliness, we may recall other temples, other sabbaths and their celebrants who have died and been reborn, who are always with us, the "communion of saints," the "cloud of witnesses."

The words of 1 Corinthians 12 also weave us into community:

> There are varieties of working, but it is the same God who inspires them all in every one. To each is given the manifestation of the Spirit for the common good. . . . As it is, there are many parts, yet one body. The eye cannot say to the hand, "I have no need of you" nor again the head to the feet, "I have no need of you." . . . But God has so adjusted the body, giving the greater honor to the inferior part, that there may be no discord in the body, but that the members may have the same care for one another. If one member suffers, all suffer together; if one member is honored, all rejoice together (6-7, 20-21, 24-26).

This passage from 1 Corinthians suggests to us that all work of the body, whether it be "women's work" (stereotypically that of the small, repeated movements of hands and feet?) or "men's work" (stereotypically that of the head and of the large movements of the arms and legs?) is to be equally valued if it is a work inspired by God for the common good. I think of the passages of Mary kneeling at Jesus' feet, once just listening, with empty hands, and once anointing, with the precious ointment in her hands; in both instances I see in my mind's eye a portrait of the work of men and women joining together as one, attending to "the one thing necessary."

Prayer and Paradox

In considering what it means to act out of the power of God in Spirit, I am still a confused Martha. I want my actions to be rooted in this power and to have effects I can identify as "good." But it is not up to me, not my prerogative, to equate an action I feel is rooted in God's power with accomplishment. My reading of David Burrell's discussion of the "Paradoxes of Action" in his book *Aquinas: God and Action* convinces me of that. He writes, "I shall show how Aquinas' paradigm for *actus*—intentional activity—in no way countenances any inherent connection between action and accomplishment" (163), and I become less confused, although mightily challenged.

When Aquinas deals with the issue of the active or the contemplative life, he uses part of our first text, Luke 10:42, "Mary has chosen the better part; it is not to be taken from her," as his central text (Burrell, 166). "What is clear," asserts Burrell, "is that Aquinas values the activity of sanctification wrought by God within the person over any action—however good—that the person may accomplish. . . . Allowing God's sanctifying action to take one over is, in fact [according to Aquinas], to fulfill one's wildest aspiration, 'because contemplation of the divine truth . . . is the end of the whole human life' " (167).

Burrell points to the "certain movements [which] appear to be more or less conducive to releasing one from the illusions of acting" and which may free one to act truly: "Such movements are embodied in traditional spiritual disciplines, and gestured at by terms like 'prayer' and 'meditation' " (171). He cites the Gospel of Mark narrative of Jesus telling his apostles, just back from a tour of villages where they had cast out unclean spirits: "Come away by yourselves to a lonely place, and rest a while" (6:30). Jesus seeks to teach a discipline which will release them from the temptation of taking credit for their "accomplishments"; they are to make a deliberate effort to turn over to God the fruits of their actions (171–172).

So, what I learn from the discussion of *actus* which Burrell offers is that contemplation, that "most 'energized' of human states," when it becomes the heart of activity paradoxically reconciles the "opposites" (174). Contemplation and its renunciation of accomplishment in action brings all our work into harmony with the power of God, channeled through earthly love.

A similar vision is sympathetically presented in a letter to a young activist from Thomas Merton:

> All the good that you will do will come not from you but from the fact that you have allowed yourself, in the obedience of faith, to be used by God's love. Think of this more, and gradually you will be free from the need to prove yourself, and you can be more open to the power that will work through you without your knowing it. . . . The real hope, then, is not in something we think we can do, but in God who is making something good out of it in some way we cannot see (Forest, 53; Merton's letter to Forest was dated 21 February 1966).

So it is that Martha and Mary within us and among us may be known as intertwined threads in this weaving; together they make a complete movement, over and under as in the plain weave, inner and outer, contemplating and acting, inspiring and expiring (acknowledging birthing, dying, and rebirthing). Together they represent the breath-weaving that is life in its wholeness, a fabric with its source in divine love and intended to honor divine will.

Martha and Mary reveal to us that we may bring to even the meanest daily tasks a spirit I find exemplified in *Brother Lawrence's Conversations and Letters on the Practice of the Presence of God*. Brother Lawrence, who must be among the humblest, most joyful members of the Household, writes: "We can do *little* things for God. I turn the cake that is frying on the pan for love of Him, and that done, if there is nothing else to call me, I prostrate myself in worship before Him, who has given me grace to work" (19). Like Brother Lawrence, we may learn simply that our sanctification does "not depend upon *changing* our works, but in doing that for God's sake which commonly we do for our own" (15).

We Are Weaving an Altar Cloth

I have written a letter which belongs here near the close of this text. It did not come to be written until long after most of the rest of the text was drafted. It leads to the conclusion which at first I could not write.

Dear Martha and Mary,

You have been my weaving/writing teachers in this work, and I thank you. I am humbled and inspired by the beauty of your service in the Household. You have set me a challenging task: to become who I most truly am in service of God. And furthermore, you challenge me to trust myself as serving in community with many other weavers—past, present, and future—whom I shall never meet but upon whose faithful work I depend.

As I've been working toward a final draft of this text, I hear your voices again; they tell me that there is one powerful lesson left for me to write about. It has to do with giving up control over what happens with the work itself, something I've talked about, mostly by quoting others, in this last chapter but have not quite been able to enact myself.

I've been holding something back. It's a quotation I found several years ago from Kierkegaard; at first I thought it was perfect for this weaving, but then I backed away from it. As you will see, it demands much in terms of presenting our work for *God's* glory and not our own.

Your lives have demonstrated to me how one may weave faith and life in a wonderful spirit of receiving and giving which does not hold back. So now I feel able at last, thanks to your teaching, to offer this text as part of my own conclusion. It represents a wholeheartedness that I saw you accepting from God in Jesus, a wholeheartedness which I yearn toward and here affirm.

May we always weave the Household together in this Spirit!

In joyful gratitude,

Nancy

Here is the passage from Kierkegaard's *Purity of Heart is to Will One Thing* which I now happily offer:

> When a woman makes an altar cloth, so far as she is able, she makes every flower as lovely as the graceful flowers of the field, as far as she is able, every star sparkling as the glistening stars of the night. She withholds nothing, but uses the most precious things she possesses. She sells off every other claim upon her life that she may purchase the most uninterrupted and favorable time of the day and night for her one and only, for her beloved work. But when the cloth is finished and put to its sacred use: then she is deeply distressed if someone should make the mistake of looking at her art, instead of at the meaning of the cloth (27).

In contemplating the "meaning of the cloth," I am reminded of a sentence one of my Coolidge Colloquium colleagues quoted in a midrash session (he said it was from the *Story of the Seven Beggars*): "Deeds of loving kindness weave the fabric of time with sparks of redemptive light."

This time of study and growth with the stories of Martha and Mary has led me to believe that such deeds rely on our keeping centered in the loving One who creates us all, whose Spirit yearns to weave us all together.

Bibliography

Atwood, Margaret. *The Handmaid's Tale.* Boston: Houghton Mifflin Co., 1986.

Baker, Aelred. "One Thing Necessary." *The Catholic Biblical Quarterly* 27 (1965) 127–37.

Brother Lawrence's Conversations and Letters on the Practice of the Presence of God. 1692. Cincinnati: Forward Movement Pubs., n.d.

Brown, Raymond E. "Roles of Women in the Fourth Gospel." *Theological Studies* 36 (December 1975) 688–699.

Burrell, David, C.S.C. *Aquinas: God and Action.* Notre Dame: Univ. of Notre Dame Press, 1979.

Campbell, Joseph, with Bill Moyers. *The Power of Myth.* Ed. Betty Sue Flowers. New York: Doubleday, 1988.

Cirlot, J. E. *A Dictionary of Symbols.* New York: Philosophical Library, 1962.

The Cloud of Unknowing and the Book of Privy Counseling. Ed. William Johnston. Garden City, N.Y.: Image Books, 1973.

Cosby, Gordon. "A Prayer of a Chance: Taking Evil Seriously." Interview by J. Wallis. *Sojourners* 15 (June 1986) 14–19.

Craighead, Meinrad. *The Mother's Songs: Images of God the Mother.* New York: Paulist Press, 1986.

Cullman, Oscar, and A. J. B. Higgins. *The Other Gospels: Non-Canonical Gospel Texts.* Ed. Ron Cameron. Philadelphia: The Westminster Press, 1982.

Daly, Mary. *Gyn/Ecology: The Metaethics of Radical Feminism.* Boston: Beacon Press, 1978.

_____. *Pure Lust: Elemental Feminist Philosophy.* Boston: Beacon Press, 1984.

"Disciple." *Encyclopedic Dictionary of the Bible.* 2d rev. ed. New York: McGraw-Hill, 1963.

Eckhart, Meister. *Breakthrough: Meister Eckhart's Creation Spirituality in New Translation.* Intro. and commentaries by Matthew Fox, O.P. New York: Image Books, 1980.

"Ecumenical." *The American Heritage Dictionary of the English Language.* Ed. William Morris. Boston: Houghton Mifflin, 1976.

Eisler, Riane. *The Chalice and the Blade: Our History, Our Future.* San Francisco: Harper & Row, 1988.

Fiorenza, Elisabeth Schüssler. *In Memory of Her: A Feminist Theological Reconstruction of Christian Origins.* New York: Crossroad, 1983.

_____. "A Feminist Critical Interpretation for Liberation: Mary and Martha: Luke 10:38-42." *Religion and Intellectual Life* 3 (Winter 1986) 21–36.

Forest, James H. "Thomas Merton's Struggle with Peacemaking." In *Thomas Merton: Prophet in the Belly of a Paradox,* ed. Gerald Twomey, 15–54. New York: Paulist Press, 1978.

Foster, Richard J. *Celebration of Discipline: The Path to Spiritual Growth.* New York: Harper & Row, 1978.

The Golden Legend of Jacobus De Voragine. Trans. Granger Ryan and Helmut Ripperger. New York: Arno Press, 1969.

Hahn, Thich Nhat. *Being Peace.* Berkeley: Parallax Press, 1987.

Haughton, Rosemary. *The Re-Creation of Eve.* Springfield, Ill.: Templegate Pubs., 1985.

Hinton, Elizabeth G. "Affirmations." *Unfolding* 1:4 (1984) 3–4.

"Hospitality" and "Host." *The American Heritage Dictionary of the English Language.* Ed. William Morris. Boston: Houghton Mifflin, 1976.

Ide, Arthur Frederick. *The Teachings of Jesus on Women.* Dallas: Texas Independent Press, 1984.

Johnson, Buffie, and Tracy Boyd. "The Eternal Weaver." *Heresies* 2 (Spring 1978) 64–69.

Jong, Erica. "The Artist as Housewife/The Housewife as Artist." In *The First MS. Reader,* ed. Francine Klagsbrun, 111–122. New York: Warner Books, Inc., 1973.

Jung, Carl Gustav. "The Stages of Life." In *The Portable Jung,* ed. Joseph Campbell and trans. R. F. C. Hull, 3–22. New York: Penguin Books, 1971.

Kierkegaard, Søren. *Purity of Heart is to Will One Thing: Spiritual Preparation for the Office of Confession.* New York: Harper & Bros., Pubs., 1948.

Knight, Gareth. *The Red Cross and the Goddess: The Quest for the Eternal Feminine Principle.* New York: Destiny Books, 1985.

A Letter of Private Direction by the Author of the Cloud of Unknowing. New York: Crossroad, 1981.

Levertov, Denise. *The Freeing of the Dust*. New York: New Directions Books, 1975.

"Line." *The American Heritage Dictionary of the English Language*. Ed. William Morris. Boston: Houghton Mifflin, 1976.

Luke, Helen M. *Woman Earth and Spirit: The Feminine in Symbol and Myth*. 1981. New York: Crossroad, 1987.

Maritain, Jacques and Raissa. *Liturgy and Contemplation*. Trans. Joseph W. Evans. New York: P. J. Kenedy and Sons, 1960.

"Mary of Bethany." *New Catholic Encyclopedia*. New York: McGraw-Hill, 1967.

May, Gerald G. *Will and Spirit: A Contemplative Psychology*. San Francisco: Harper & Row, 1982.

Merton, Thomas. *What is Contemplation?* Springfield, Ill.: Templegate Pubs., 1978.

Moltmann-Wendel, Elisabeth. *The Women Around Jesus*. New York: Crossroad, 1982.

Neumann, Erich. *The Great Mother: An Analysis of the Archetype*. 2d ed., trans. Ralph Mannheim. 1955. Princeton: Princeton Univ. Press, 1974.

Nomura, Yoshi. *Desert Wisdom: Sayings From the Desert Fathers*. Garden City, N.Y.: Image Books, 1984.

Ochs, Carol. *Women and Spirituality*. Totowa, N.Y.: Rowman & Allanheld, 1983.

The Oxford Annotated Bible with the Apocrypha: Revised Standard Version. Eds. Herbert G. May and Bruce M. Metzger. New York: Oxford Univ. Press, 1965.

Palmer, Parker. *To Know as We Are Known: A Spirituality of Education*. San Francisco: Harper & Row, 1983.

————. *The Active Life: A Spirituality of Work, Creativity, and Caring*. San Francisco: Harper & Row, 1990.

Purtle, Carol. *The Marian Paintings of Jan Van Eyck*. Princeton: Princeton Univ. Press, 1982.

Reifler, Sam. *I Ching: A New Interpretation for Modern Times*. New York: Bantam, 1974.

Rotenberg, Mordechai. *Dialogue With Deviance: The Hasidic Ethic and the Theory of Social Contraction*. Philadelphia: Institute for the Study of Human Issues, 1983.

The R.S.V. Interlinear Greek-English New Testament. The Nestle Greek Text with a Literal English Translation by The Rev. Alfred Marshall D. Litt. Grand Rapids, Mich: Zondervan Pub. House, 1968.

Russell, Kate. "Kate Russell: Weaving the Structure of Life." *FiberArts* 12:4 (July/August 1985) 11.

Shaler, Nathaniel Southgate. Excerpt from *The Autobiography of*

Nathaniel Southgate Shaler. Here and Now II. Ed. Fred Morgan. New York: Harcourt, Brace, Jovanovich, 1972.

Shoemaker, Lorna. "Martha and Mary: A Study in Wholeness." *Concern* (January 1984) 5-7.

Silko, Leslie Marmon. "Language and Literature From a Pueblo Perspective." In *English Literature: Opening Up the Canon,* ed. Leslie A. Fiedler and Houston A. Baker, 54-72. Baltimore and London: Johns Hopkins Univ. Press, 1981.

Spretnak, Charlene. *Lost Goddesses of Early Greece.* Boston: Beacon Press, 1984.

Stoneburner, Tony. "Letting One Thing Lead to Another." *Religion and Intellectual Life* 1 (Summer 1984) 90-102.

Swidler, Leonard. "Jesus Was a Feminist." *Catholic World* 212 (1971) 177-83.

Talbert, Charles H. *Reading Luke: A Literary and Theological Commentary on the Third Gospel.* New York: Crossroad, 1982.

Tedlock, Barbara and Dennis. "Text and Textile: Language and Technology in the Arts of the Quiché Maya." *Journal of Anthropological Research* 41 (Summer 1985) 121-146.

Temple, William. *Readings in St. John's Gospel.* London: Macmillan & Co., Ltd., 1950.

Tetlow, Elizabeth Meier. *Women and Ministry in the New Testament.* New York: Paulist Press, 1980.

Thoreau, Henry David. *Walden and Other Writings of Henry David Thoreau.* Ed. Brooks Atkinson. New York: The Modern Library, 1950.

Tillich, Paul. *The New Being.* New York: Charles Scribner's Sons, 1955.

"Tissue." *The American Heritage Dictionary of the English Language.* Ed. William Morris. Boston: Houghton Mifflin, 1976.

Ulanov, Ann and Barry. *Primary Speech: A Psychology of Prayer.* Atlanta: John Knox Press, 1982.

Underhill, Evelyn. *The House of the Soul and Concerning the Inner Life.* 1929. Minneapolis: Seabury Press, 1984.

_____. *Mixed Pasture; Twelve Essays and Addresses.* 1933. Reprint. Freeport, N.Y.: Books for Libraries Press, 1968.

Walker, Barbara G. *The Woman's Encyclopedia of Myths and Secrets.* San Francisco: Harper & Row, 1983.

"Weave." *The Oxford English Dictionary.* 2d ed. Vol. 20:63. Oxford: Clarendon Press, 1989.

"Weaving." *Encyclopaedia Britannica.* Encyclopaedia Britannica, Inc.: Chicago, 1970.

Wolkstein, Diane and Samuel Noah Kramer. *Inanna: Queen of Heaven and Earth: Her Stories and Hymns From Sumer.* New York: Harper & Row, 1983.